Microsoft® Excel 2000®
Brief Edition

INTERACTIVE COMPUTING SERIES

Kenneth C. Laudon
Kenneth Rosenblatt

Azimuth Interactive, Inc.

Boston   Burr Ridge, IL   Dubuque, IA   Madison, WI   New York   San Francisco   St. Louis
Bangkok   Bogotá   Caracas   Lisbon   London   Madrid   Mexico City   Milan   New Delhi   Seoul
Singapore   Sydney   Taipei   Toronto

McGraw-Hill Higher Education ❦

*A Division of The **McGraw-Hill** Companies*

MICROSOFT EXCEL 2000 BRIEF EDITION
Copyright © 2000 by The McGraw-Hill Companies, Inc. All rights reserved. Printed in the United States of America. Except as permitted under the United States Copyright Act of 1976, no part of this publication may be reproduced or distributed in any form or by any means, or stored in a data base or retrieval system, without the prior written permission of the publisher.

 This book is printed on recycled, acid-free paper containing 10% postconsumer waste.

2 3 4 5 6 7 8 9 0 QPD/QPD 9 0 9 8 7 6 5 4 3 2 1 0 9

ISBN   0-07-234076-2

Vice president/Editor-in-Chief: *Michael W. Junior*
Sponsoring editor: *Trisha O'Shea*
Developmental editor: *Kyle Thomes*
Senior marketing manager: *Jodi McPherson*
Project manager: *Carrie Sestak*
Production supervisor: *Michael R. McCormick*
Senior freelance design coordinator: *Laurie Entringer*
Supplement coordinator: *Matthew Perry*
Compositor: *Azimuth Interactive, Inc.*
Typeface: *10/12 Sabon*
Printer: *Quebecor Printing Book Group/Dubuque*

Library of Congress Catalog Card Number: 99-62388

http://www.mhhe.com

Microsoft® Excel 2000®
Brief Edition

INTERACTIVE COMPUTING SERIES

Kenneth C. Laudon
Kenneth Rosenblatt

Azimuth Interactive, Inc.

At McGraw-Hill Higher Education, we publish instructional materials targeted at the higher education market. In an effort to expand the tools of higher learning, we publish texts, lab manuals, study guides, testing materials, software, and multimedia products.

At Irwin/McGraw-Hill (a division of McGraw-Hill Higher Education), we realize technology will continue to create new mediums for professors and students to manage resources and communicate information with one another. We strive to provide the most flexible and complete teaching and learning tools available and offer solutions to the changing world of teaching and learning.

Irwin/McGraw-Hill is dedicated to providing the tools necessary for today's instructors and students to navigate the world of Information Technology successfully.

Seminar Series - Irwin/McGraw-Hill's Technology Connection seminar series offered across the country every year, demonstrates the latest technology products and encourages collaboration among teaching professionals.

Osborne/McGraw-Hill - A division of the McGraw-Hill Companies known for its best-selling Internet titles *Harley Hahn's Internet & Web Yellow Pages* and the *Internet Complete Reference*, offers an additional resource for certification and has strategic publishing relationships with corporations such as Corel Corporation and America Online. For more information, visit Osborne at www.osborne.com.

Digital Solutions - Irwin/McGraw-Hill is committed to publishing Digital Solutions. Taking your course online doesn't have to be a solitary venture. Nor does it have to be a difficult one. We offer several solutions, which will let you enjoy all the benefits of having course material online. For more information, visit www.mhhe.com/solutions/index.mhtml.

Packaging Options - For more about our discount options, contact your local Irwin/McGraw-Hill Sales representative at 1-800-338-3987, or visit our Web site at www.mhhe.com/it.

Interactive Computing Series

Goals/Philosophy

The *Interactive Computing Series* provides you with an illustrated interactive environment for learning software skills using Microsoft Office. The Interactive Computing Series is composed of both text and multimedia interactive CD-ROMs. The text and the CD-ROMs are closely coordinated. *It's up to you. You can choose how you want to learn.*

Approach

The *Interactive Computing Series* is the visual interactive way to develop and apply software skills. This skills-based approach coupled with its highly visual, two-page spread design allows the student to focus on a single skill without having to turn the page. A running case study is provided through the text, reinforcing the skills and giving a real-world focus to the learning process.

About the Book

The Interactive Computing Series offers *two levels* of instruction. Each level builds upon the previous level.

Brief lab manual - covers the basics of the application, contains two to four chapters.
Introductory lab manual - includes the material in the Brief textbook plus two to four additional chapters. The Introductory lab manuals prepare students for the *Microsoft Office User Specialist Proficiency Exam (MOUS Certification)*.

Each lesson is organized around **Skills**, **Concepts**, and **Steps (Do It!)**.

Each lesson is divided into a number of Skills. Each **Skill** is first explained at the top of the page.
Each **Concept** is a concise description of why the skill is useful and where it is commonly used.
Each **Step (Do It!)** contains the instructions on how to complete the skill.

About the CD-ROM

The CD-ROM provides a unique interactive environment for students where they learn to use software faster and remember it better. The CD-ROM is organized in a similar approach as the text: The **Skill** is defined, the **Concept** is explained in rich multimedia, and the student performs **Steps (Do It!)** within sections called Interactivities. There are at least 45 Interactivities per CD-ROM. Some of the features of the CD-ROM are:

Simulated Environment - The Interactive Computing CD-ROM places students in a simulated controlled environment where they can practice and perform the skills of the application software.
Interactive Exercises - The student is asked to demonstrate command of a specific software skill. The student's actions are followed by a digital "TeacherWizard" that provides feedback.
SmartQuizzes - Provide performance-based assessment of the student at the end of each lesson.

Using the Book

In the book, each skill is described in a two-page graphical spread (Figure 1). The left side of the two-page spread describes the skill, the concept, and the steps needed to perform the skill. The right side of the spread uses screen shots to show you how the screen should look at key stages.

Figure 1

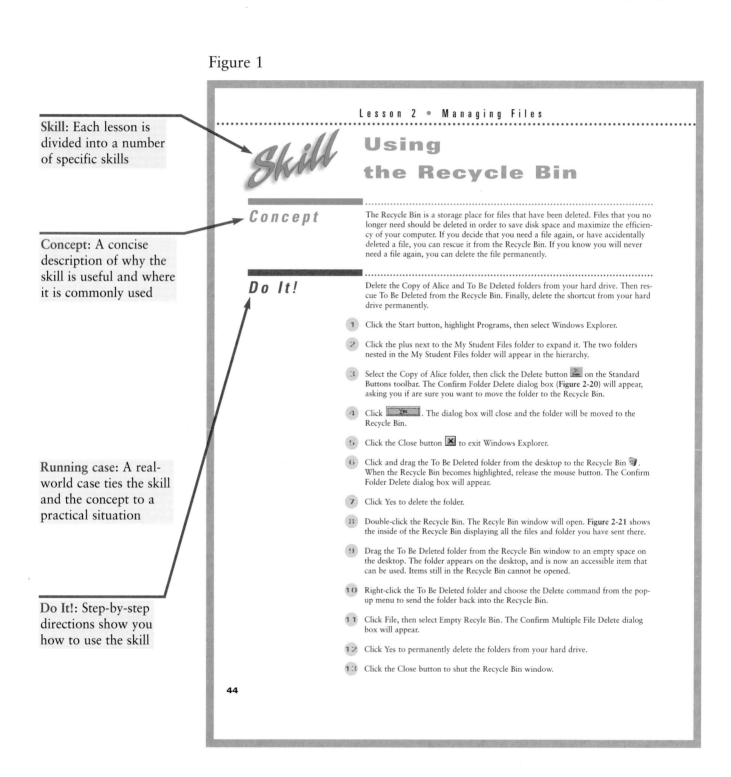

Skill: Each lesson is divided into a number of specific skills

Concept: A concise description of why the skill is useful and where it is commonly used

Running case: A real-world case ties the skill and the concept to a practical situation

Do It!: Step-by-step directions show you how to use the skill

---

Lesson 2 • Managing Files

Skill
Using the Recycle Bin

Concept

The Recycle Bin is a storage place for files that have been deleted. Files that you no longer need should be deleted in order to save disk space and maximize the efficiency of your computer. If you decide that you need a file again, or have accidentally deleted a file, you can rescue it from the Recycle Bin. If you know you will never need a file again, you can delete the file permanently.

Do It!

Delete the Copy of Alice and To Be Deleted folders from your hard drive. Then rescue To Be Deleted from the Recycle Bin. Finally, delete the shortcut from your hard drive permanently.

1. Click the Start button, highlight Programs, then select Windows Explorer.

2. Click the plus next to the My Student Files folder to expand it. The two folders nested in the My Student Files folder will appear in the hierarchy.

3. Select the Copy of Alice folder, then click the Delete button 🗙 on the Standard Buttons toolbar. The Confirm Folder Delete dialog box (**Figure 2-20**) will appear, asking you if are sure you want to move the folder to the Recycle Bin.

4. Click ___Yes___. The dialog box will close and the folder will be moved to the Recycle Bin.

5. Click the Close button 🗙 to exit Windows Explorer.

6. Click and drag the To Be Deleted folder from the desktop to the Recycle Bin 🗑. When the Recycle Bin becomes highlighted, release the mouse button. The Confirm Folder Delete dialog box will appear.

7. Click Yes to delete the folder.

8. Double-click the Recycle Bin. The Recyle Bin window will open. **Figure 2-21** shows the inside of the Recycle Bin displaying all the files and folder you have sent there.

9. Drag the To Be Deleted folder from the Recycle Bin window to an empty space on the desktop. The folder appears on the desktop, and is now an accessible item that can be used. Items still in the Recycle Bin cannot be opened.

10. Right-click the To Be Deleted folder and choose the Delete command from the pop-up menu to send the folder back into the Recycle Bin.

11. Click File, then select Empty Recyle Bin. The Confirm Multiple File Delete dialog box will appear.

12. Click Yes to permanently delete the folders from your hard drive.

13. Click the Close button to shut the Recycle Bin window.

44

End-of-Lesson Features

In the book, the learning in each lesson is reinforced at the end by a quiz and a skills review called Interactivity, which provides step-by-step exercises and real-world problems for the students to solve independently.

INTERACTIVE COMPUTING • Windows 98

Windows 98

More

Table 2-1 Ways to delete or restore a selected file

TO DELETE	TO RESTORE
Click the Delete button on the toolbar	Click the Undo button on the toolbar
Right-click and select Delete from the pop-up menu	Right-click the file in the Recycle Bin and select Restore
Drag the file to the Recycle Bin	Drag the file from the Recycle Bin to any location
Press [Delete]	Go to the File menu in the Recycle Bin and select Restore

Summary tables: Tables give you a quick overview of shortcuts and toolbar icons needed to use the skills

Figure 2-20 Confirm Folder Delete dialog box

Click No to cancel move to Recycle Bin

Screen shots: Screen shots show you what the screen should like after following the Do It! steps

Figure 2-21 Recycle Bin window

Deleted items in Recycle Bin

Space occupied on hard drive by deleted items; empty Recycle Bin to recover space

Number of items in Recycle Bin

Practice

Move the shortcut you created in the last skill to the Recycle Bin. Then move the shortcut out of the Recycle Bin and back to the desktop. Delete the shortcut a second time using a different technique. This time, delete the shortcut permanently.

Hot Tip

Files can be erased immediately without being stored in the Recycle Bin. Right-click the Recycle Bin, then select Properties. On the View tab, uncheck the "Display delete confimation dialog box" command. This enables you to delete files in one step.

Hot Tip: Gives you advice on how to use the software and warns you of potential problems

45

Practice: Allows you to practice the skill with a built-in exercise or directs you to a student file

Using the Interactive CD-ROM

The Interactive Computing multimedia CD-ROM provides an unparalleled learning environment in which you can learn software skills faster and better than in books alone. The CD-ROM creates a unique interactive environment in which you can learn to use software faster and remember it better. The CD-ROM uses the same lessons, skills, concepts, and Do It! steps as found in the book, but presents the material using voice, video, animation, and precise simulation of the software you are learning. A typical CD-ROM contents screen shows the major elements of a lesson (see Figure 2 below).

Skills list: A list of skills allows you to jump directly to any skill you want to learn or review, including interactive sessions with the TeacherWizard

Figure 2

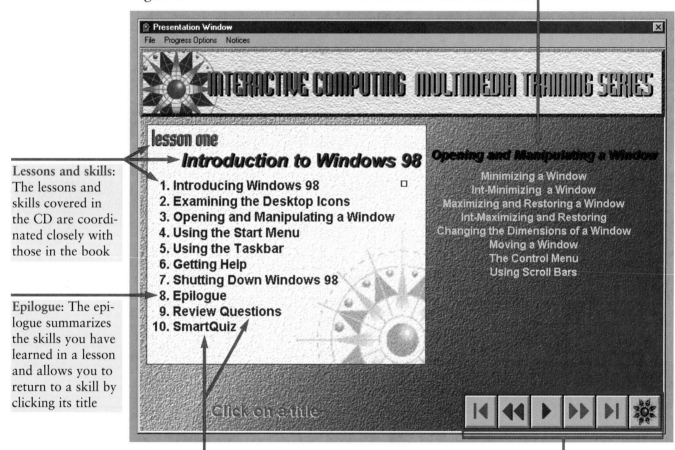

Lessons and skills: The lessons and skills covered in the CD are coordinated closely with those in the book

Epilogue: The epilogue summarizes the skills you have learned in a lesson and allows you to return to a skill by clicking its title

Review Questions and SmartQuiz: Review Questions test your knowledge of the concepts covered in the lesson; SmartQuiz tests your ability to accomplish tasks in a simulated software environment

User controls: Precise and simple user controls permit you to start, stop, pause, jump forward or backward one sentence, or jump forward or backward an entire skill. A single navigation star takes you back to the lesson's table of contents

Unique Features of the CD-ROM: TeacherWizard™ and SmartQuiz™

Interactive Computing: Software Skills offers many leading-edge features on the CD currently found in no other learning product on the market. One such feature is *interactive exercises* in which you are asked to demonstrate your command of a software skill in a precisely simulated software environment. Your actions are followed closely by a digital TeacherWizard that guides you with additional information if you make a mistake. When you complete the action called for by the TeacherWizard correctly, you are congratulated and prompted to continue the lesson. If you make a mistake, the TeacherWizard gently lets you know: "No, that's not the right icon. Click on the Folder icon on the left side of the top toolbar to open a file." No matter how many mistakes you make, the TeacherWizard is there to help you.

Another leading-edge feature is the end-of-lesson SmartQuiz. Unlike the multiple choice and matching questions found in the book quiz, the SmartQuiz puts you in a simulated digital software world and asks you to show your mastery of skills while actually working with the software (Figure 3).

Figure 3

SmartQuiz: For each skill you are asked to demonstrate, the SmartQuiz monitors your mouse and keyboard actions

Skill question: Interactive quiz questions correspond to skills taught in lesson

Automatic scoring: At the end of the SmartQuiz, the system automatically scores the results and shows you which skills you should review

Teaching Resources

The following is a list of supplemental material available with the Interactive Computing Series:

ATLAS Active Testing and Learning Assessment Software - available for the Interactive Computing Series, is our cutting edge "Real TimeAssessment" software. ATLAS is web-enabled and allows students to perform timed tasks while working live in an application. ATLAS will track how a specific task is completed and the time it takes to complete that task. ATLAS measures Proficiency and Efficiency ("It's not only what you do but how you do it."). ATLAS will provide full customization and authoring capabilities for professors, and includes content from all of our application Series.

Instructor's Resource Kits

The Instructor's Resource Kit provides professors with all of the ancillary material needed to teach a course. Irwin/McGraw-Hill is dedicated to providing instructors with the most effective instruction resources available. Many of these resources are available at our Information Technology Supersite www.mhhe.com/it. Our Instructor's Kits are available on CD-ROM and contain the following:

Network Testing Facility (NTF) - Tests acquired software skills in a safe simulated software environment. NTF tracks a student score and allows the instructor to build screens that indicate student progress.

Diploma by Brownstone - is the most flexible, powerful, and easy-to-use computerized testing system available in higher education. The diploma system allows professors to create an Exam as a printed version, as a LAN-based Online version, and as an Internet version. Diploma includes grade book features, which automate the entire testing process.

Instructor's Manual - Includes:
-Solutions to all lessons and end-of-unit material
-Teaching Tips
-Teaching Strategies
-Additional exercises.

Student Data Files - To use the Interactive Computing Series, students must have Student Data Files to complete practice and test sessions. The instructor and students using this text in classes are granted the right to post the student files on any network or stand-alone computer, or to distribute the files on individual diskettes. The student files may be downloaded from our IT Supersite at www.mhhe.com/it.

Series Web Site - Available at www.mhhe.com/cit/apps/laudon.

Digital Solutions

Pageout Lite - is designed if you're just beginning to explore Web site options. Pageout Lite is great for posting your own material online. You may choose one of three templates, type in your material, and Pageout Lite instantly converts it to HTML.

Pageout - is our Course Web site Development Center. Pageout offers a Syllabus page, Web site address, Online Learning Center Content, online exercises and quizzes, gradebook, discussion board, an area for students to build their own Web pages, and all the features of Pageout Lite. For more information please visit the Pageout Web site at www.mhla.net/pageout.

OLC/Series Web Sites - Online Learning Centers (OLCs)/Series Sites are accessible through our Supersite at www.mhhe.com/it. Our Online Learning Centers/Series Sites provide pedagogical features and supplements for our titles online. Students can point and click their way to key terms, learning objectives, chapter overviews, PowerPoint slides, exercises, and web links.

The McGraw-Hill Learning Architecture (MHLA) - is a complete course delivery system. MHLA gives professors ownership in the way digital content is presented to the class through online quizzing, student collaboration, course administration, and content management. For a walk-through of MHLA visit the MHLA Web site at www.mhla.net.

Packaging Options - For more about our discount options, contact your local Irwin/McGraw-Hill Sales representative at 1-800-338-3987 or visit our Web site at www.mhhe.com/it.

Visit www.mhhe.com/it
THE ONLY SITE WITH ALL YOUR CIT AND MIS NEEDS.

Acknowledgments

The Interactive Computing Series is a cooperative effort of many individuals, each contributing to an overall team effort. The Interactive Computing team is composed of instructional designers, writers, multimedia designers, graphic artists, and programmers. Our goal is to provide you and your instructor with the most powerful and enjoyable learning environment using both traditional text and new interactive multimedia techniques. Interactive Computing is tested rigorously in both CD and text formats prior to publication.

Our special thanks to Trisha O'Shea and Kyle Lewis, our Editors for computer applications and concepts. Both Trisha and Kyle have poured their enthusiasm into the project and inspired us all to work closely together. Kyle Thomes, our Developmental Editor, has provided superb feedback from the market and excellent advice on content. Jodi McPherson, marketing, has added her inimitable enthusiasm and market knowledge. Finally, Mike Junior, Vice-President and Editor-in-Chief, provided the unstinting support required for a project of this magnitude.

The Azimuth team members who contributed to the textbooks and CD-ROM multimedia program are:

Ken Rosenblatt (Textbooks Project Manager and Writer, Interactive Writer)
Raymond Wang (Interactive Project Manager)
Russell Polo (Programmer)
Michele Faranda (Textbook design and layout)
Jason Eiseman (Technical Writer)
Michael Domis (Technical Writer)
Larry Klein (Contributing Writer)
Thomas Grande (Editorial Assistant, layout)
Stefon Westry (Multimedia Designer)

Contents

Contents

Continued

L E S S O N

INTRODUCTION TO SPREADSHEET SOFTWARE

Microsoft Excel is a computer application that improves your ability to record data and then extract results from it. With Excel, you can enter text labels and numerical values into an electronic spreadsheet, a grid made up of columns and rows. The computerized worksheets you work with in Excel resemble handwritten ledgers with which you may already be familiar. Being able to use spreadsheet software can help you both professionally and personally. By providing an organized structure in which to work, Excel can increase the efficiency with which you conduct business and track your own affairs. Excel's ability to perform and automate calculations saves time and decreases the possibility of error.

Using Excel, you will learn how to create a spreadsheet employing proper design techniques. You will then explore the application and become familiar with its basic elements and operations. Later on, some of Excel's more advanced features such as formulas, What-if analysis, and macros will broaden your knowledge of how to create and work with a spreadsheet. If you need assistance while using Excel, the program includes an extensive help facility, as well as the ability to access online support via the World Wide Web.

CASE STUDY
Kay Samoy is the owner of a small but successful company that distributes a wide variety of dog accessories such as treats, furnishings, and toys. She would like to use Excel to track her income, expenses, and profits electronically now that her business is growing. Kay will begin by familiarizing herself with the application. Then she will take the first steps toward creating an effective spreadsheet.

Introducing Excel and Worksheet Design

Concept

Microsoft Excel is an electronic spreadsheet application designed to make the creation and use of professional quality spreadsheets fast and easy. A **spreadsheet** is a table composed of rows and columns that store text and numbers for easy viewing and tabulation. Electronic spreadsheets are very useful for performing rapid and accurate calculations on groups of interrelated numbers. Using Excel, you can:

- Organize information rapidly and accurately. With the proper data and formulas, Excel calculates your results automatically.

- Recalculate automatically. Fixing errors in Excel is easy. When you find a mistake and correct the entry, Excel automatically recalculates all related data.

- Keep track of the effect that changing one piece of data has on related numbers. You can postulate changes that may occur in the future and see how they could change the results of your calculations – a feature called **What-If** analysis.

- Display data as graphs or charts. Excel allows you to display numeric data graphically in the form of charts that are automatically updated as the data changes. For example, **Figure 1-1** shows the data in a spreadsheet for income and expenditures that can also be displayed in the form of a pie chart. Charts often make relationships among data easier to understand.

The spreadsheet's organization is shaped by its goal or purpose. A well-designed spreadsheet should be accurate, easily understood, and should include the four sections visible in **Figure 1-2**: documentation, assumptions, input, and results.

- The first section contains **documentation**, consisting of a complete description of the name of the author, the purpose of the spreadsheet, the date it was created, and the name of the spreadsheet file. Documentation should also specify location of any cell ranges and macros. Ranges are blocks of columns and rows that are useful for performing certain types of calculations and for displaying data. Macros are instructions for automating spreadsheet tasks.

- The second section of a spreadsheet is used to display **assumptions**. Assumptions are variable factors that may change in a worksheet. For example, Kay's profit projections assume that sales will expand by 10% each quarter. When her sales numbers are changed, they will affect the amount of profit. It is easier to change documented assumptions than undocumented ones. Assumptions are useful when conducting "what-if" analysis based on calculating the effect of changes in spreadsheet data. For instance, what if sales only grow by 5%? You will learn more about What-If analysis in Lesson 2.

- The third section of the spreadsheet stores **input**, the numbers that you enter and manipulate. In **Figure 1-2**, the input section contains data for income and expenditures. Input data is generally arranged in blocks of numbers organized in columns and rows.

- The fourth section is a **results**, or output section, which displays the results of the calculations made on the input data. Output data is generally placed below and to the right of input data.

More

Microsoft Excel stores each workbook you create as an individual document in the computer's memory. A document, also called a file, can be a single worksheet or may contain many of pages of data and graphs. Each file should be given a unique name so it can be easily differentiated from other files. Excel documents are given the file extension .xls. A file extension is a three letter code, separated from the file name with a period, called a dot, that tells the computer what application is associated with a particular file.

Figure 1-1 A worksheet made with Microsoft Excel

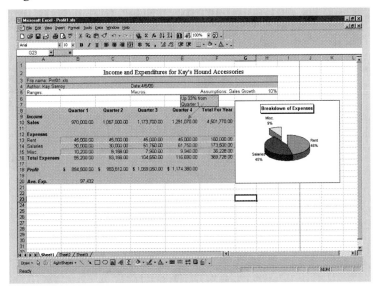

Figure 1-2 Organization of a spreadsheet

Hot Tip

An electronic spreadsheet application, such as Excel, allows you to easily share data between worksheets or with another application so that it need not be entered again.

Starting Excel

Concept

To use the Microsoft Excel program, or application, the user must first open it. The act of opening an application can also be called running, starting, or launching. In the Windows environment, you can launch a program in a number of ways, including using desktop and Start menu shortcuts, using the Run command, double-clicking executable file icons, and clicking a Windows 98 Quick Launch toolbar button.

Do It!

Kay wants to open the Microsoft Excel application so she can begin to construct a worksheet.

1 Make sure the computer, monitor and any other necessary peripheral devices are turned on. The Windows desktop should appear on your screen. Your screen may differ slightly from the one shown.

2 Locate the Windows taskbar, usually found at the bottom of your screen. Use the mouse to guide the pointer over the Start button, on the left side of the taskbar, and click ⬛Start . This will open the Windows Start menu.

3 Move the mouse pointer ⍫ up the Start menu to Programs, highlighting it. The Programs menu will be displayed as shown in **Figure 1-3**.

4 Position the pointer over Microsoft Excel to highlight it, and then click once to open the application. (If Excel is not there, try looking under Microsoft Office on the Start menu.) Excel will open with a blank worksheet in the window as shown in **Figure 1-4**.

More

Each computer can vary in its setup depending on its hardware and software configurations. Therefore, your Excel startup procedure may be slightly different from that described above. The Windows environment allows you to place shortcuts to a program's executable (.exe) file in various places. For example, the Excel listing on the Programs menu is a shortcut. You can also place shortcuts on the desktop, or even on the first level of the Start menu. Because you can customize the Excel program your screen may not look exactly like the one shown to the right.

Figure 1-3 Windows desktop and Start menu

Start menu

Programs menu

Start button

Taskbar

Excel 2000

Figure 1-4 Excel window

Office Assistant

Hot Tip

The Office Assistant shown in the figure above is part of the Excel help facility and will be discussed in detail later in this Lesson.

Exploring the Excel Screen

Concept

In order to begin building a spreadsheet it is necessary to become familiar with the Excel window and worksheet elements.

Do It!

To familiarize herself with the Excel screen, Kay will click on various elements of the window.

1 Click the Maximize button ▣, located at the right side of the title bar, to enlarge the Excel window so that it fills your entire screen. The title bar at the top of the Excel window displays the name of the program and the title of the current worksheet that is open. When Excel opens, it automatically creates a new, empty worksheet file called Book1. The title bar also houses the Minimize ▬, Maximize ▣ or Restore ▣, and Close buttons ✕ used to resize the window. The Minimize button reduces the window to its program button on the taskbar. The Maximize button will appear if the Excel window has not been enlarged to fill the entire screen, and the Restore button, which returns the window to its previous size and location, will appear if the window is maximized. Double-clicking the title bar will also maximize or restore a window.

2 Click File to open the File menu, then guide the pointer over each menu to familiarize yourself with the different commands. The main menu bar is usually displayed right below the title bar. The menu bar contains lists with most of Excel's commands. Each word in the menu bar can be clicked to open a pull-down menu of commands. Or, a menu may be opened by pressing the Alt key and the underlined letter in the menu name. The menu bar also contains a set of sizing buttons. These controls function in the same manner as the application sizing buttons, only they apply to the active workbook window, not the entire Excel program. You can have more than one workbook window open in the Excel program window.

3 Move the pointer over the New button ▣. A brief description of the button's function, a ScreenTip, will appear in a small rectangle below the button. Guide the pointer over the toolbars, pausing on each button to read its description, as shown in **Figure 1-5**. The two rows of icons beneath the menu bar are called toolbars. Toolbar buttons provide shortcuts to many of Excel's most commonly used commands. You can customize the toolbars to contain the tools that you use most often. The top toolbar in **Figure 1-5** is called the Standard toolbar, and the lower toolbar is called the Formatting toolbar.

4 Click the Select All button, the gray rectangle in the upper-left corner of the worksheet where the row and column headings meet. The entire worksheet becomes highlighted, and the row and column heading buttons will become depressed. The worksheet is where you enter data to create your spreadsheet. A spreadsheet can contain many worksheets, and together multiple worksheets make up a workbook.

More

The Standard toolbar and Formatting toolbar are just two of the many toolbars available in Excel. To view and activate additional toolbars, open the View menu from the menu bar and highlight the Toolbars command. A submenu of toolbar names will appear. Click a toolbar to activate it. Excel toolbars are flexible objects. You can anchor them to any side of the Excel window by clicking and dragging, or float them over the middle of the Excel screen. If all the buttons associated with a particular toolbar do not fit on the toolbar due to window or screen size, a small arrow button will appear at the end of the toolbar. Click on the arrow to reveal a menu of the remaining buttons.

You may have noticed that the Excel window contains two sets of sizing buttons. The top set, in the window's title bar, controls the Excel application window. The bottom set controls the active Excel document.

Excel 2000

Figure 1-5 Elements of the Excel application window

Title bar

Menu bar

Standard toolbar

Formatting toolbar

Select All button

Cell pointer

Sizing buttons

Exploring the Excel Screen (continued)

Do It!

5 Click the letter A that heads the first column. Column A becomes highlighted, as shown in **Figure 1-6**. The columns are designated by letters, from A to Z, then AA to AZ and so on up to IV, altogether making 256 columns.

6 Click the number 1 at the left of the first row. Row 1 becomes highlighted. The rows are labeled numerically down the left side of the worksheet, from 1 to 65,536.

7 Click the intersection of column D and row 7. Cell D7 is now active. Excel designates the active cell on the worksheet by bordering it with a dark rectangle called a cell pointer. Rows intersect with columns forming the grid system. Each intersection of a row and a column is called a cell. Cells are identified by an address composed of the letter and number of the column and row that intersect to form the cell. When a cell is active, you can enter new data into it or edit any data that is already there. You can make another cell active by clicking it, or by moving the cell pointer with the arrow keys found on the keyboard.

8 Click cell H9. Below the second row of icons are the name box and the formula bar. The name box displays the active cell address, H9, and the formula bar displays the data that you are working on, along with its location on the worksheet. The formula bar is now blank.

9 Double-click cell H9. At the bottom of the Excel screen is the status bar, which changes in response to the task in progress. As Figure 1-7 shows, "Enter" should now appear in the status bar indicating that you can enter a label, data, or a formula into the cell. The left side of this bar displays a brief description of Excel's current activities. The boxes to the right indicate the status of particular keys, such as the Caps Lock key.

10 Click the down arrow on the vertical scroll bar to move the spreadsheet down one row, hiding row 1. The vertical scroll bar on the far right side of the worksheet window and the horizontal scroll bar on the lower edge of the worksheet window help you move quickly around the worksheet.

11 Below the active worksheet, Excel provides Sheet tabs that you can click to switch to other worksheets in the open workbook. Click the Sheet 2 tab. Notice that the cell pointer moved from H9, the active cell on Sheet 1, to cell A1, the active cell on Sheet 2. Related worksheets can be arranged together in workbooks. Book 1 in the title bar actually stands for Workbook 1. Workbooks can contain up to 255 worksheets. Sheet tab scrolling buttons (in the lower-left corner of the window) help you view worksheet tabs not in the window.

Figure 1-6 Selecting a column

Column A heading button

Row 1 heading button

Mouse pointer

Cell D7

Excel 2000

Figure 1-7 Components of the Excel application window

Insertion point

I-beam

Vertical scroll bar

Sheet tab

Horizontal scroll bar

Status bar

Practice

To practice what you have learned in this Skill, click the Minimize button on the menu bar to minimize the document window and display it as a small title bar at the bottom of the window. Then click its Maximize button to enlarge the document.

Hot Tip

The document and application control menu icons, at the left end of the menu and title bars respectively, offer menus containing the Close and sizing commands.

Moving Around the Worksheet

Concept

To effectively use Excel you must be able to maneuver between cells in the workspace. To do this you may either use the mouse or the keyboard, depending on your personal preference or your current activity. For example, if you are entering a large quantity of data quickly into cells that are close together, it may be easier and more efficient to use the keyboard. If you need to select a cell that is far from the active cell, using the mouse would probably be more effective.

Do It!

Kay moves to various points on the Excel worksheet to familiarize herself with Excel's navigation.

1 Using the mouse, move the mouse pointer ✛ to cell **B4** and click the left mouse button. The cell becomes highlighted, marking it as the active cell.

2 Press [◄]. The cell pointer moves over one cell to the left to **A4**.

3 Press [▲]. The cell pointer moves up one cell to **A3**.

4 Press the [►], then [▼] to return the cell pointer to cell **B4**.

5 Click once on the arrow at the right end of the horizontal scroll bar. The worksheet will scroll right by one column.

6 Scroll down one row by clicking once on the arrow at the bottom vertical scroll bar.

7 Click the horizontal scroll bar arrow until column **Z** is visible. Notice that the scroll bar box shrinks to allow you a larger movement area, as seen in **Figure 1-8**.

8 Click and hold the mouse button on the horizontal scroll bar box. You have now grabbed the box. Drag the box to the left until you can see column **A**.

Figure 1-8 Getting around the Excel application window

Name box displays selected cell, B4, even though it is not currently visible

Row 4 button bold, indicating that a cell in that row is selected

Column names extend past Z and begin again with AA, AB, etc.

Horizontal scroll bar box

Moving Around the Worksheet (continued)

Do It!

9 Click **Edit**, then select **Go To**. The Go To dialog box, shown in **Figure 1-9**, appears. The Go To command is useful when you have to move a great distance across the worksheet.

10 At the bottom of the dialog box there is a text box, the white area with a flashing insertion point, labeled **Reference**. Type **Y95** in the Reference text box.

11 Click [Open]. Excel's cell pointer highlights cell Y95 in the worksheet.

12 Press [Ctrl]+[Home]. The cell pointer will jump to cell A1. The [Ctrl]+[Home] command is helpful for returning to the beginning of a worksheet.

More

At the bottom of the worksheet are three **tabs** labeled Sheet1, Sheet2, and Sheet3. A workbook is often made up of many **worksheets,** and each tab corresponds to a different worksheet. Interrelated data can be kept across multiple worksheets of the same workbook for viewing, cross referencing, and calculation. To go to a different worksheet, simply click its tab at the bottom of the window. New worksheets can be added to a workbook by using the Worksheet command on the Insert menu. The new worksheet will appear before the active worksheet. You can move a worksheet to a different place in the worksheet hierarchy by dragging its tab to the desired place in the row of tabs. The mouse pointer will appear with a blank sheet attached to it 🖳 and a small arrow ▼ will indicate where the worksheet will be placed when you release the mouse button. The tab scrolling buttons ◀◀ ▶▶ , located to the left of the sheet tabs, allow you to view tabs that do not fit in the window. Clicking one of the outer buttons moves you to the beginning or end of the list of tabs, while clicking one of the inner buttons will move you through the tabs one at a time. If you right-click the tab scrolling buttons, a pop-up menu listing all of the tabs in your workbook will appear, allowing you to select a specific tab to jump to. Tabs can be renamed by double-clicking the tab to select its text, and then editing it like normal text. Right-clicking a tab opens a shortcut pop-up menu with commands that allow you to rename, delete, insert, and copy or move a worksheet.

Table 1-1 Moving in a Worksheet

MOVEMENT	ACTION
Left one cell	Press [←] or [Shift]+[Tab]
Right one cell	Press [→] or [Tab]
Up one cell	Press [↑] or [Shift]+[Enter]
Down one cell	Press [↓] or [Enter]
Left one column or right one column	Click the left arrow or right arrow on the horizontal scroll bar
Up one row or down one row	Click the up arrow or down arrow on the vertical scroll bar.
Up one screen or down one screen	Press [Page Up] or [Page Down]
Left one screen or right one screen	Press [Alt]+[Page Up] or [Alt]+[Page Down]
Go to cell A1	[Ctrl]+[Home]
Go to colum A in current row	[Home]

Figure 1-9 Go To dialog box

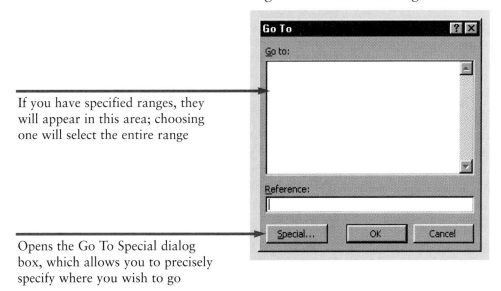

If you have specified ranges, they will appear in this area; choosing one will select the entire range

Opens the Go To Special dialog box, which allows you to precisely specify where you wish to go

Practice

Click cell E12 to make it active, then use the arrow keys to move the cell pointer to cell G7. Open the Go To dialog box and navigate to cell CT2041. Finally, position the cell pointer in cell A1.

Hot Tip

To move across a large area of blank cells press [End], the word END will appear in the status bar, then press an arrow key. The cell pointer will jump to the next filled cell in the direction of the arrow key pressed.

Entering Labels

Concept

Labels are used to annotate and describe the data you place into rows and columns. Properly labeled data makes your spreadsheet easy to understand and interpret. Labels can consist of text or numbers and are aligned left so as to differentiate them from data used in calculations. Excel automatically left-justifies labels. Labels should be entered into your spreadsheet first so that your rows and columns are defined before your begin to enter the calculable data.

Do It!

Kay enters the documentation and row labels for her spreadsheet.

1 Click cell A2 to make it the active cell. The address A2 appears in the name box.

2 Type Income and Expenditures for Kay's Hound Accessories, then click the Enter button ✔. The label will appear in the formula bar as you type. Even though the label is longer than the cell width, it will be displayed in its entirety as long as the next cell remains empty.

3 Click cell A3 and type File name: Profit1.xls, then press [Enter]. The label will be entered and the cell pointer will move down one row to cell A4.

4 Type Author: Kay Samoy, click cell D4 and type Date: 4/6/00. In cell A5 type Ranges:, in cell D5 type Macros:, and in cell F5 type Assumptions: Sales Growth. These labels are the documentation for your spreadsheet. Documentation describes and titles your spreadsheet. It contains the purpose, file name and author of the spreadsheet, the date it was created, as well as defining any ranges, macros and assumptions that it may contain.

5 Click cell A8 to make it the active cell. Type Income and then press [Enter]. The next six labels will be the row headings.

6 Type Sales, then press [Enter]; skip a cell and in cell A11 type Expenditures, then press [Enter]; in cell A12 type Rent, then press [Enter]; in cell A13 type Salaries, then press [Enter]; in cell A14 type Misc., then press [Enter]; and in cell A15 type Total Expenses, then press [Enter]. Your worksheet should now look like the one shown in **Figure 1-10**.

More

Then Enter button on the formula bar functions in much the same way as the Enter key on the keyboard, but after you click the Enter button, the cell pointer remains in the current cell instead of moving to the cell beneath. The Enter button disappears after you use it, but you can bring it back by clicking the text box on the formula bar. The Cancel button ✖ not only removes the contents from a cell, but also restores the cell's previous contents, if there were any.

Excel automatically assumes that a number is a value and aligns it to the right by default. If you wish to use a number as a label, simply type an apostrophe ['] before the number. The data will then be aligned to the left. The apostrophe will be hidden in the cell, but will be shown in the formula bar.

Figure 1-10 Entering labels

Documentation section

Labels aligned left

Practice

Click the **New** button ☐ to open a new workbook. Beginning in cell A2, enter the following information as cell labels, pressing **[Enter]** after each: your name, today's date, your instructor's name, and the title of this course.

Hot Tip

If you start to enter a label whose first few letters match those of an adjacent cell in the column, Excel will automatically complete the label to match. If you do not wish to accept the suggestion, simply continue typing to overwrite Excel's suggestion.

Saving and Closing a Worksheet

Concept

Saving your work is important; if not saved, work can be lost due to power or computer failure. Once a file has been saved, it can be reopened at any time for editing or viewing. Your workbook can be saved to a hard drive, floppy disk, network drive, or even a Web server. Closing a file removes it from the screen and puts it away for later use. You can close a file while leaving the application open for use with other Excel files. Or, if you are finished using Excel, you can exit the application.

Do It!

Kay wants to save her worksheet under the name Profit1 in a folder titled Kay's Hound Accessories.

1 Click Window, then select Book1.xls from the menu if it is not already active. Book1.xls will become the active document.

2 Click File, then click Save As. Notice that the Save As command is followed by an ellipsis (three dots), indicating that a dialog box will open when the command is executed. The Save As dialog box opens, as shown in **Figure 1-11**. (If you had chosen the Save command, the Save As dialog would have appeared anyway, as this is the first time you will be saving your document.) The file name Book1.xls automatically appears highlighted in the File Name text box, ready to be changed.

3 To give the workbook file a more distinctive name, type Profit1. The .xls file extension will automatically be added. As you type the name, Book1.xls will be overwritten. Windows 95 and 98 support file names of up to 255 characters. The file name can contain uppercase or lowercase letters, numbers, and most symbols.

4 Click the Save in list arrow to choose where to save the file. Excel is programmed to save newly created files in the My Documents folder by default. Click 3½ Floppy (A:) if your student files will be stored on a floppy disk or Maindisk (C:) if your student files are to be stored on your hard drive. Consult your instructor if you have any doubts about this matter.

5 Click the Create New Folder button 🗁. The New Folder dialog box will appear with the folder name New Folder highlighted in the Name: text box, as shown in **Figure 1-12**.

Figure 1-11 Save As dialog box

Click to return to the save location you selected previously

Click to create a new folder in the currently selected directory

Buttons allow you to select common storage locations quickly

Click to move one level up in your file hierarchy

Click to reveal a list of file formats in which the file may be saved

Excel 2000

Figure 1-12 New Folder dialog box

Future location of folder being created

Saving and Closing a Worksheet (continued)

Do It!

6 Type Kay's Hound Accessories. The default name will be replaced with the new text.

7 Click ⬜ OK ⬜. The new folder will be created and opened automatically in the Save As dialog box. The contents window will be blank since there are no files or folders in Kay's folder, as shown in **Figure 1-13**.

8 Click 🖫 Save to store the worksheet in Kay's folder. The Save As dialog box will close and the new file name will appear in the Excel window's title bar.

9 Click File, then click Close. The workbook file is removed from the Excel window.

More

You can also use the **AutoSave** option to have Excel automatically save your file every few minutes. The AutoSave command is found on the **Tools** menu. If it is not there, you will have to install the AutoSave add-in. Select the **Add-Ins** command from the Tools menu to open the Add-Ins dialog box. Click the check box next to AutoSave, and then click the OK button. After Excel has set up the AutoSave feature, select it from the Tools menu; the AutoSave dialog box, shown in **Figure 1-14**, will open. You can turn AutoSave on or off with the check box at the top-left of the dialog box, and you can choose the time between saves by entering an interval in the text box labeled minutes. You have the option of saving just the active workbook or all of the open workbooks, and Excel can prompt you before it auto saves if you wish, so as to avoid inadvertently saving unwanted changes.

Understanding the difference between the Save command and the Save As command is an important part of working with most software. When you save a new file for the first time, the two commands function identically; they both open the Save As dialog box, allowing you to choose a name and storage location for the file. Once you have saved a file, the commands serve different purposes. Choosing the Save command will update the original file with any changes you have made, maintaining the same file name and location. Choosing the Save As command will permit you to save a different version of the same file, with a new name, location, or both.

Figure 1-13 Saving a file in a new folder

New folder
selected in
Save in: box

Click to open a
menu of advanced
dialog box options

Click to put icons
in a different view

Default file name
given by Excel

Click to open
your Web
browser to a
search page

Figure 1-14 AutoSave dialog box

Use this check box
to turn AutoSave
on or off

Check here to require
confirmation before
AutoSave operates

Excel 2000

Practice

Save the workbook you created in the
Practice for the previous Skill on your student disk as Practice1-7 and then close the
workbook.

Hot Tip

The Save button 🖫 on the Standard toolbar and the keyboard combination [Ctrl]+[S]
are shortcuts to the Save command.

EX 1.19

Opening a Worksheet

Concept

In order to work with a saved file you must first open it. Opening a file requires that you know the file's name and the location in which it is stored.

Do It!

Kay needs to open her file so that she can edit one of the labels.

1 Click File, then click Open. Notice that the Open command is followed by an ellipsis (three dots) indicating that a dialog box will open, as the command requires more information. The Open dialog box will appear as shown in **Figure 1-15**.

2 Earlier you saved the file Profit1 in a folder named Kay's Hound Accessories. Click the Look in drop down list arrow and select the drive where your student files are stored. Insert your Student Disk into the A: drive and click the 3½ Floppy (A:) if they are stored on a floppy, or click Maindisk (C:) if they are in a folder on your hard disk. A list of the files and folders on the drive will appear in the list box.

3 Click the folder named Kay's Hound Accessories to select it, and then click the Open button. The files housed in the folder will appear in the contents window.

4 Double-click the Profit1 file. The Open dialog box disappears and the worksheet will be displayed in the Excel window. Notice that the cell pointer is in the same cell it was in when you last saved the worksheet.

More

If you cannot remember the name of storage location of a particular file that you need to open, Excel provides a powerful search facility that can help you. Click the Tools button in the Open dialog box and then choose the **Find** command from the menu that appears as shown in **Figure 1-16**. The Find dialog box, shown in **Figure 1-17**, will open. From the Find dialog box, you can search any drive or folder accessible from your computer for a file. You can conduct your search using a wide variety of properties including file name, the date the file was last modified, or even the name of the person who created it. Each property has its own set of conditions that you can apply to the search. For example, the File name property allows you to find a file whose name includes, begins with, or ends with a specific character or combination of characters. You submit this value in the Value text-entry box. Use the selection and text-entry boxes at the bottom of the dialog box to set your criteria, and then click the **Find Now** button to initiate the search. If your search is successful, the file you requested will be selected in the Open dialog box. Once you have run a successful search, you can save it in case you ever need to locate that file again.

The Open button in the Open dialog box includes an arrow on its right edge. Clicking this arrow opens a menu that provides commands for opening a file in a number of different ways. For example, the **Open Read-Only** command permits you to view a file, but prohibits you from saving changes to it. The **Open Copy** command creates a copy of the file you are opening and opens the copy instead. The **Open in Browser** command opens HTML files in your Web browser rather than in Excel.

Figure 1-15 Open dialog box

Open button is inactive because no files or folders are selected

Excel 2000

Figure 1-16 Find command

Figure 1-17 Find dialog box

Enter search criteria in this row of boxes

Practice

To practice opening Excel documents, open the student file **Practice-Lesson 1.xls**. Then save it to your student disk as **MyPractice 1**.

Hot Tip

When conducting a file search, activate the Search subfolders check box to ensure that you the search includes all folders in a particular location on just the top-level of the folder or drive you selected.

Editing a Cell's Information

Concept

Many spreadsheet documents are used over a long period of time and undergo constant updating. Information entered into a cell is not permanent. You can change, or edit, the contents of cell at any time. Editing the contents of a cell is very similar to editing text in a word processing document.

Do It!

Kay wants to edit cell A11 to change Expenditures to Expenses.

1. Click cell **A11**. The cell pointer moves to cell A11 and Expenditures is displayed in the formula bar.

2. Move the mouse pointer from the worksheet to the formula bar and position it between the **n** and the **d** of the word **Expenditures** (the pointer will change from a cross ✛ to an I-beam I) and click. A blinking insertion point will appear, the formula bar buttons will be displayed, and the mode indicator on the status bar will read Edit, as shown in **Figure 1-18**.

3. Click and hold the left mouse button, then drag the I-beam to the right, over the last seven letters of the word **Expenditures**. The rest of the formula bar will become highlighted. Highlighting, or selecting, text allows it to be edited.

4. Type **ses** and then click the **Enter** button ✓. The new text will replace the incorrect label and the spreadsheet will look like **Figure 1-19**.

5. Save your workbook by clicking the **Save** button 🖫.

More

Excel provides you with multiple ways to edit a cell's information. You can select the cell you wish to edit and then click the formula bar, as described above. You may also double-click a desired cell, making a flashing insertion point appear. Then you can use the backspace and/or delete keys to remove the character to the left or right of the insertion point respectively, and enter new characters to edit the cell. Or, you can double-click a second time to highlight all of the cell's contents and edit the selection. Finally, you can select a cell and then press [F2], again making the insertion point appear in the selected cell.

Figure 1-18 Editing a cell label

Place the insertion point with the mouse

Contents of the selected cell appear above in the formula bar

Indicates that Excel is in edit mode, allowing you to change the contents of the selected cell

Excel 2000

Figure 1-19 Changed cell label

Expenditures has been changed to Expenses

Using the Office Assistant

Concept

Even the most experienced computer users need help from time to time. The Office Assistant provides several methods for getting help in Excel. You can choose from a list of topics that the Assistant suggests based on the most recent functions you have performed. You can also view tips related to your current activity. Or, you can ask a question in plain English. The Office Assistant will reply with several help topics related to your question.

Do It!

Kay has a question about the Office Assistant. She will use the Office Assistant to get help.

1 If the Office Assistant is not active, click 🔲 on the Standard toolbar. The Assistant and its dialog balloon appear asking what you would like to do. Click the text box that reads **Type your question here, and then click Search**. The text will be replaced by an insertion point.

2 In the text box, type **How do I hide the Office Assistant?** and then click Search . A list of topics appears in the balloon, as shown in **Figure 1-20**.

3 Click the first topic, **Show, hide, or turn off the Office Assistant**. **Figure 1-21** shows the Microsoft Excel Help window that appears.

4 Read the Help topic pertaining to the Office Assistant.

5 When you have finished reading about the Office Assistant's capabilities, click the **Close** 🗙 button in the upper-right corner of the window.

More

From time to time the Assistant will offer you tips on how to use Excel more efficiently. The appearance of a small light bulb, either next to the Assistant or on the Office Assistant button, indicates that there is a tip to be viewed. To see the tip, click the light bulb in whichever location it appears.

The Office Assistant can be customized. Click the Options button in its dialog balloon to open the Office Assistant dialog box. This dialog box has two tabs: Gallery and Options. The **Gallery** tab contains different assistant characters you can install, and scrolling through the characters provides you with a preview of each one. From the **Options** tab, shown in **Figure 1-22**, you can control the Assistant's behavior and capabilities, and decide what kinds of tips it will show. You can also access Office Assistant commands by right-clicking the Assistant itself.

If your computer is properly connected to a printer, you can print the text of any help topic. Simply click the Print button 🖨 at the top of the help window to open the Print dialog box.

Figure 1-20 Assistant's search results

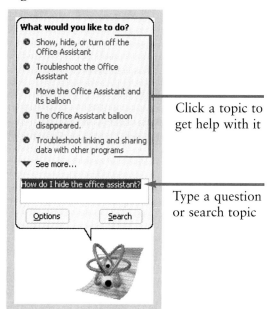

Click a topic to
get help with it

Type a question
or search topic

Figure 1-21 Help with the Office Assistant

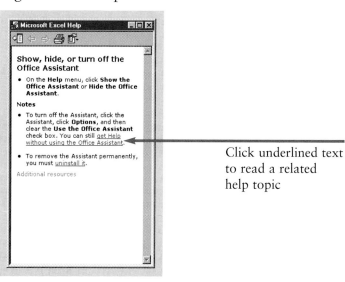

Click underlined text
to read a related
help topic

Excel 2000

Figure 1-22 Office Assistant dialog box

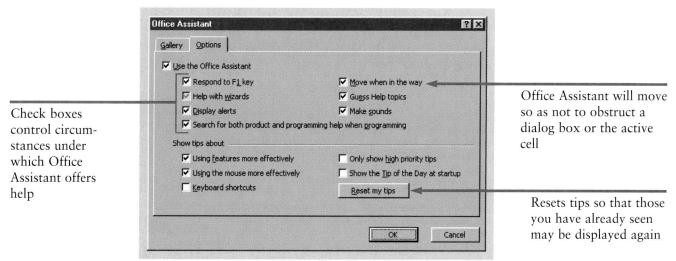

Check boxes
control circum-
stances under
which Office
Assistant offers
help

Office Assistant will move
so as not to obstruct a
dialog box or the active
cell

Resets tips so that those
you have already seen
may be displayed again

Practice

Use the Office Assistant to learn about
moving the Office Assistant and its balloon.

Hot Tip

The Office Assistant is common to all
Office 2000 applications. Therefore, any
Assistant options you change will affect it
in all Office programs.

Other Excel Help Features

Concept

Working with new software can be confusing, and, at times, even intimidating. Fortunately, Microsoft Excel offers a number of built-in help features in addition to the Office Assistant that you can use when you encounter problems or just have a question about a particular aspect of the program. The What's This? command and the Help tabs are two such features.

Do It!

Kay will use the What's This? command to get more information about the Name Box, and the Help tabs to find out more about keyboard shortcuts.

1. Click Help on the menu bar, then click What's This?. A question mark will be added to the mouse pointer ▯?. With this pointer, you can click many Excel features to receive a ScreenTip that explains them.

2. Click the Name Box. A ScreenTip like the one in **Figure 1-23** will appear to explain the item you clicked. Read the tip, and then click the mouse to erase it.

3. Click the Office Assistant (activate the feature from the Help menu first, if necessary). Click any help topic or tip the Assistant is currently offering.

4. When the Help window for that topic appears, click the Show button ▮ . The window will expand to a two-paneled format. The left panel consists of three tabs while the right panel is used to display selected help files.

5. Click the Index tab to bring it to the front of the panel if it is not already there.

6. Click in the text-entry box labeled Type keywords:, and then type keyboard. Notice that the list box in the middle of the tab scrolls automatically to match your entry.

7. When you see the word keyboard appear in the list box, double-click it. After a moment, the help topics related to keyboard will be displayed in the box at the bottom of the tab.

8. Find Keyboard shortcuts in the Choose a topic list box (you may have to scroll down) and click it. The Keyboard shortcuts help file will be loaded into the right panel of the window as shown in **Figure 1-24**.

9. Close the Help window when you finish working with it.

More

The Index tab of the Help Topics dialog box is very helpful if you know what the task you are trying to accomplish is called, or if you know the name of the feature that you want to explore. If you are unsure of exactly what you are looking for, the Contents tab may be a better option for you. The Contents tab contains every Help topic that Excel offers, broken down by category, and is useful if you wish to obtain a broad view of the topics available. It is organized like an outline or the table of contents you might find in a book. It begins with general topics, symbolized by book icons, each of which can be expanded to reveal more specific and focused subtopics. Once you have revealed a general topic's subtopics, you can select a subtopic in the left panel to display it in the right panel, just as on the Index tab. The Answer Wizard tab replicates the Office Assistant, allowing you to request help topics by entering questions in your own words. Once you have clicked the Show button to display the Help tabs in a Help window, the button changes to the Hide button. Click the Hide button to collapse the window back to a single panel.

Excel 2000

Figure 1-23 Name Box What's This? ScreenTip

Name box

The box at the left end of the formula bar that identifies the selected cell, chart item, or drawing object. Type the name in the **Name** box, and then press ENTER to quickly name a selected cell or range. To move to and select a previously named cell, click its name in the **Name** box.

Figure 1-24 Using the Help tabs

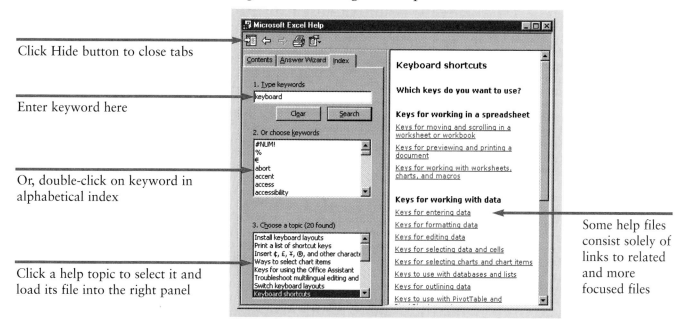

Click Hide button to close tabs

Enter keyword here

Or, double-click on keyword in alphabetical index

Click a help topic to select it and load its file into the right panel

Some help files consist solely of links to related and more focused files

Practice

Use the Index to find shortcut keys that relate to the Office Assistant.

Hot Tip

If your computer is connected to the Internet, you can access Microsoft's Web pages directly from Excel. Open the Help menu and click **Office on the Web** to launch your Web browser and go directly to the Office Web site.

Exiting Excel

Concept

It is important to exit the Excel program properly when you are finished with the day's work session. Closing the application correctly will help you avoid data loss.

Do It!

Kay has finished using Excel for the day and is ready to exit the application.

1 Click **File**, then click **Close**. Since you have altered the spreadsheet since the last time you saved, a dialog box will open asking if you want to save changes in Profit1.xls.

2 Click ⟦ Yes ⟧. Excel will save the changes you have made and the worksheet will disappear from the window.

3 To close the application click **File**, then click **Exit** (see **Figure 1-25**). Excel closes and removes itself from the desktop.

More

There are other ways you can close a file and exit Excel. The easiest method is to use the **Close** buttons ⊠ located in the upper-right corner of the window. The Close button on the menu bar is for the active workbook, and the Close button on the title bar is for the application.

You may open any menu on the menu bar by pressing the [Alt] key followed by the underlined letter in the menu's title. You will notice that menu commands also have a letter in their name underlined; typing the underlined letter will activate its command on the open menu. For example, with the File menu open, typing [c] will close the file and pressing [x] will exit Excel. If you have more than one workbook open in Excel, the program will allow you to save changes to all of them at once before closing.

Figure 1-25 Closing the Excel application

Clicking this Close button will likewise exit the application

Practice

Open Excel, and then Exit the application by clicking the Close button ⊠ on the title bar.

Hot Tip

Pressing the **[Ctrl]** key plus **[W]** will close your file, while **[Alt] + [F4]** is the key combination used to exit Excel.

Shortcuts

Function	Button/Mouse	Menu	Keyboard
Create a new file	▢	Click File, then click New	[Ctrl]+[N]
Open a file	📂	Click File, then click Open	[Ctrl]+[O]
Maximize a window	▢	Click Control icon, then click Maximize	
Minimize a window	▬	Click Control icon, then click Minimize	
Restore a window	▣	Click Control icon, then click Restore	
Close a window	✕	Click Control icon, then click Close	[Alt]+[F4] (application) [Ctrl]+[W] (document)
Confirm a cell entry	✓		[Enter], [Tab], Arrow keys
Cancel a cell entry	✕	Click Edit, then click Undo typing	[Ctrl]+[Z]
Search the Web (from the Open dialog box)	🔍		
Save a file	💾	Click File, then click Save	[Ctrl]+[S]
Office Assistant	?	Click Help, then click Microsoft Excel Help	[F1]
What's This?	? In a dialog box	Click Help, then click What's This?	[Shift]+[F1]

Identify Key Features

Name the items identified by callouts in **Figure 1-26**.

Figure 1-26 Elements of the Excel screen

Excel 2000

Select The Best Answer

10. Click this to make the Excel window fill the screen

11. Displays the active cell address

12. Displays a brief description of your current activities in Excel

13. Allows you to choose a name and location for storing a file

14. Saves your file keeping its current name and location

15. Answers your questions and offers guidance as you work

16. Allows you to search for a file from the Open dialog box

17. Location where you can edit the contents of a cell

a. Name Box

b. Office Assistant

c. Maximize button

d. Find command

e. Save As command

f. Formula bar

g. Save button

h. Status bar

Complete the Statement

18. To select an entire column, click:

    a. The first cell in the column

    b. Any cell in the column

    c. Its letter column heading

    d. The corresponding row number

19. Text or numbers that describe your data are called:

    a. Annotations

    b. Ranges

    c. Justifications

    d. Labels

20. Pressing [Ctrl]+[Home] will:

    a. Move your view up one screen

    b. Move your view down one screen

    c. Move the cell pointer to cell A1

    d. Move the cell pointer to Column A in the current row

21. All of the following actions will move the cell pointer to another cell except:

    a. Clicking the Enter button

    b. Pressing the Enter key

    c. Pressing the Tab key

    d. Pressing an Arrow key

22. A well-designed spreadsheet does not require:

    a. Documentation

    b. Multiple worksheets

    c. Input

    d. Output

23. All of these are Excel Help features except:

    a. The Index tab

    b. The Office Assistant

    c. What's This?

    d. The HelpWizard

24. A file extension:

    a. Allows you to see a hidden file

    b. Lets you edit the information in a cell

    c. Associates a file with a specific application

    d. Is part of Excel's Help facility

25. A workbook can contain:

    a. 16 worksheets

    b. 255 worksheets

    c. 3 worksheets

    d. 65, 536 worksheets

26. Excel assumes that numbers entered on the worksheet are:

    a. Values

    b. Labels

    c. Formulas

    d. Apostrophes

Interactivity

Test Your Skills

1. Open the Excel application and document a new spreadsheet:

   a. Use the Start button to launch Microsoft Excel.

   b. Add a documentation section to the blank worksheet using the title **Class Schedule**, your name, and the date.

   c. When you document the file name, use the name **Test 1.xls**.

   d. Include labels for ranges and macros. Your documentation section should occupy Rows 1-4 of the worksheet.

2. Design a worksheet that displays your daily class schedule:

   a. Add labels in Row 6 for the days of the week. Start in cell B6, and skip a column between each day. **Friday** should be in cell J6.

   b. Add labels in Column A for your class periods. Enter the time of your earliest class in cell A8, and then add a label for each subsequent class period through your last class of the day. Skip a row between each time label.

   c. Enter the names of your classes in the appropriate cells where the day of the week and the time intersect.

3. Get help from the Office Assistant:

   a. Open the Office Assistant's dialog balloon.

   b. Ask the Assistant for information on how to **customize toolbars**.

   c. Choose a topic that the Assistant provides, and then read the information in the Help window.

   d. Close the Help window when you are done, and then close the Office Assistant's window.

4. Save your file and exit Excel:

   a. Save your spreadsheet under the name **Test 1.xls**.

   b. Exit Microsoft Excel.

Interactivity (continued)

Problem Solving

1. Create a new spreadsheet following the design principles you learned in Lesson 1. Design this spreadsheet to log your daily activities. Enter labels for the days of the week just as you did in the previous exercise, but this time add Saturday and Sunday after Friday, and do not leave a blank column between each day. Instead of class periods, add labels down Column A for **Class, Activities, Meals, Studying/Homework, Leisure,** and **Sleep.** Do not skip rows between labels. Save the file as Solved 1-1.xls.

2. Due to a recent merger, your accounting firm can now increase the budgets of several departments. You are elated to learn that you will have an additional $10,000 available for your expense account. As a member of the Human Resources department, you know how much this money will help you attract the top candidates for your company's job openings. Use Excel to design a spreadsheet that will detail your strategy for utilizing the new funds over the next year. You do not have to enter any monetary values yet. Simply set up the structure of the worksheet with labels. Save the file as **Solved-HR.xls.**

3. At your urging, the restaurant you manage has just purchased a new computer complete with Office 2000. The owner of the restaurant, who was reluctant to make the purchase, wants you to prove that it was a sound investment. Using Excel, design a spreadsheet that will allow you to keep track of the waitstaff's schedule over one week. Your worksheet should include columns for **Time In** and **Time Out** each day of the week. Save the file as **Solved-Rest.xls.**

L E S S O N

2

MANIPULATING DATA IN A WORKSHEET

One of the greatest advantages of using spreadsheet software is that it automates many of the processes that take up so much time when done by hand. In Excel, you can move or copy data from one location in a worksheet to another quickly and easily.

Excel also automates your calculations by using mathematical formulas. If you instruct Excel what operation to perform, and where to get the data, the program will execute the calculations for you. The Paste Function feature prevents you from having to enter complicated formulas that Excel already knows. Once you have entered a formula or a function, you can even paste it into a new location.

Often, businesses like to use the data they have gathered to make projections about their business. In Excel, you can use assumptions to perform calculations under different conditions, altering the results of the worksheet each time. This technique is known as What-if analysis, and takes full advantage of Excel's versatility.

CASE STUDY
In this lesson, Kay will use Excel's Cut, Copy, and Paste features to manipulate the labels in her spreadsheet. She will also fill out the worksheet with values, and then use those values to perform calculations using formulas and functions. Then she will change her output by performing a What-If analysis. Finally, Kay will print a copy of her worksheet.

Cutting, Copying, and Pasting Data

Concept

Excel makes it easy to transfer data from cell to cell. **Cutting** or **Copying** information places it on the **Office Clipboard**, a temporary storage place for data. If you have used the Windows operating system or previous versions of Microsoft Excel before, you may be familiar with the Windows Clipboard. The Office Clipboard can hold up to 12 items at once, while the Windows Clipboard holds only one. The two Clipboards are related in the following ways: the last item you sent to the Office Clipboard can also be found on the Windows Clipboard; when you clear the Office Clipboard the Windows Clipboard is erased as well. Both Clipboards are volatile. That is, they are erased automatically when you shut down your computer. The **Paste** command inserts the last item you sent to the Clipboard at the insertion point. Cell contents may also be moved by dragging and dropping with the mouse.

Do It!

Kay wants to add the column heading **Quarter** in four cells, B6, C6, D6, and E6 of her spreadsheet. Then she will cut and paste the column headings from row 6 to row 7.

1 Open Excel by clicking the **Start** button, then selecting **Excel** from the Programs menu. The Excel window will appear on your desktop.

2 Click the Open button ![icon], then find the folder named Kay's Hound Accessories, and open **Profit1.xls**. Your workbook will appear in the Excel window.

3 Click cell **B6**. The cell pointer will appear in cell B6 to indicate it is active.

4 Type **Quarter**, then click the **Enter** button ![icon] to confirm the entry. The label will appear in cell B6.

5 Click **Edit**, then click **Copy** to send a duplicate of the contents of the selected cell to the Clipboard. An animated dashed border appears around the copied selection, as shown in **Figure 2-1**.

6 Press [Tab] to move the cell pointer to cell **C6**. Notice that the animated border remains in cell B6.

7 Click **Edit**, then click **Paste** to insert the copied text into the selected cell.

8 Move the mouse pointer to the fill handle, the black square in the lower-right corner of the cell, until it changes to a crosshair **✚** indicating that the selection can be copied elsewhere in the document.

9 Click the left mouse button and drag the fill pointer to cell **E6**. The cells will appear with a gray border, identifying them as a possible destination for the copied data, and a ScreenTip displaying the text to be copied will appear, as seen in **Figure 2-2**.

10 Release the mouse button. A copy of the selected data will appear in cells D6 and E6.

Figure 2-1 Copying a cell

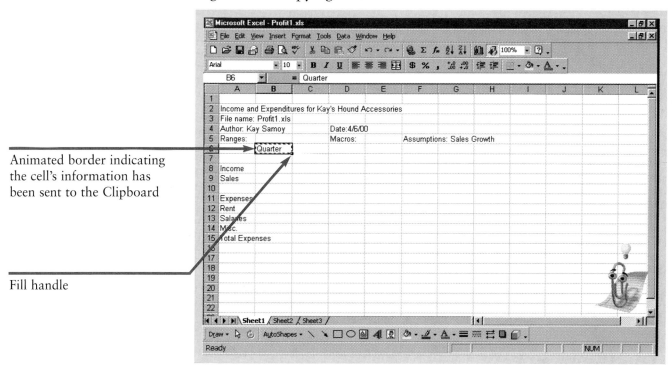

Animated border indicating the cell's information has been sent to the Clipboard

Fill handle

Excel 2000

Figure 2-2 Selected destination cells

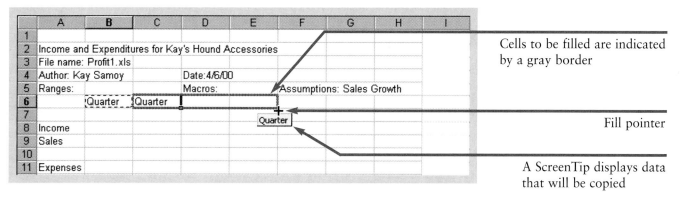

Cells to be filled are indicated by a gray border

Fill pointer

A ScreenTip displays data that will be copied

Cutting, Copying, and Pasting Data (continued)

Do It!

11 Double-click cell B6 to put it into edit mode. Edit will appear in the status bar.

12 Place the I-beam after Quarter, press [Space], then type [1]. The label will read Quarter 1.

13 Repeat the previous steps so that cells C6 through E6 read Quarter 2 thorough 4 respectively. Your worksheet should now resemble the one in **Figure 2-3**.

14 Click cell B6 to select it, then drag the mouse pointer to cell E6 so that all four cells are encompassed in the cell pointer. Cells C6, D6, and E6 will be highlighted.

15 Click the Cut button 🔏 on the Standard toolbar. The column headings are surrounded by an animated border.

16 Click cell B7, then drag to cell E7 to select the entire group as the destination cells for the cut information.

17 Click the Paste button 🔲. The column headings in row 6 will be pasted into row 7, as shown in **Figure 2-4**.

18 Save your worksheet by clicking the Save button 🔲.

More

You can move or copy a cell's contents with the mouse by dragging and dropping. Dragging involves positioning the pointer over an object, clicking the left mouse button to grab the object, and then moving the mouse, and the object, to a new location. When the mouse pointer is over a cell pointer it will change to an arrow. You can then click and drag the cell pointer to a new location to move the contents of the selected cell or cells without having to use the Clipboard. Releasing the mouse button drops a grabbed object into place. Pressing [Ctrl] while dragging and dropping causes the pointer to change to the copy pointer ⌖. When dropped, the contents of the selection will appear in the new location but the original information will remain intact.

If you want to fill a range of cells with copies of a selected cell or cells, move the mouse pointer to the **fill handle**, the square at the bottom-right corner of a cell pointer, until it changes to a crosshair. Then click and drag the mouse pointer in the direction of the columns or rows that you wish to fill; a gray border will appear around the cells which will be filled with copies of your original selection when you release the mouse button. Using the fill handle allows you to make multiple copies of a selected cell or range's content at the same time, whereas you can only make a single copy of a cell or range's content using the drag-and-drop method described above.

As stated earlier, you can store up to 12 items on the Office Clipboard. To paste an item other than the one you cut or copied most recently, open the View menu, highlight Toolbars, and click Clipboard on the submenu that appears. The Clipboard toolbar, shown in **Figure 2-5**, will open. The Clipboard toolbar allows you to choose exactly which stored item you want to paste. Point to an icon on the toolbar to receive a ScreenTip that tells you what piece of data the icon represents.

Figure 2-3 Edited cells

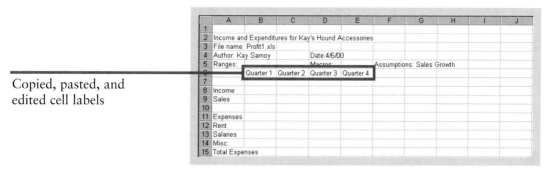

Copied, pasted, and
edited cell labels

Figure 2-4 Cut and pasted cells

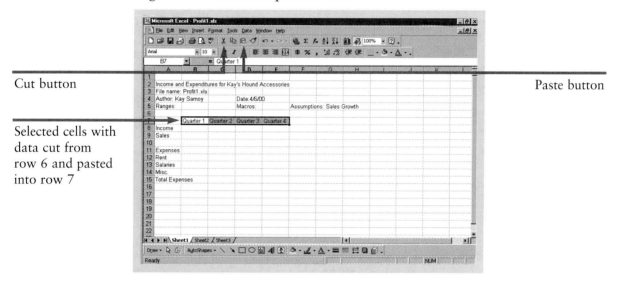

Cut button

Paste button

Selected cells with
data cut from
row 6 and pasted
into row 7

Figure 2-5 Office Clipboard

Click an icon to select
the piece of stored data
it represents, then select
Paste command

Click to clear Office (and
Windows) Clipboard

Practice

Open the practice file **Practice-Lesson
2.xls**, save it as **MyPractice2**, and then follow the instructions on the **Prac2-1** sheet.

Hot Tip

The Cut command removes the contents of
a cell and sends them to the Clipboard. The
Copy command sends a copy of a cell's
content to the Clipboard, leaving the original data in the cell.

Entering Values

Concept

Values are numbers, formulas or functions that Excel uses in calculations. They must be entered and confirmed in the same way that labels are.

Do It!

Kay wants to enter sales and expense values into her worksheet.

1. Click cell **B9** to make it the active cell.

2. Type 970000, then press [Tab]. The first quarter sales value is entered into the cell and the cell pointer moves to the right to cell C9.

3. Now enter the rest of the Sales values in the row, pressing [Tab] after each: 1000400, 1210305, 1484032.

4. Click cell **B12** to activate it.

5. Type 45000 and then click the Enter button ✅.

6. Since the rent is the same for each quarter, copy the data in cell **B12** and paste it into the other three cells in the row; C12, D12, and E12, by clicking on the fill handle, dragging it to cell **E12**, and then releasing it. Notice the ScreenTip that shows the data that will be copied.

7. Click cell **B13** to activate it and enter the following four values into the Salaries row, pressing [Tab] after each: 30000, 30000, 51750, 61750.

8. Click cell **B14** to activate it and enter the following four Misc. values into the row, pressing [Tab] after each: 10200, 8188, 7900, 9940. Your worksheet should now resemble the one shown in **Figure 2-6**.

More

You may have noticed that the values you entered, unlike labels, were aligned to the right when confirmed. Excel aligns values to the right by default and recognizes an entry as a value when it is a number or it is preceded by +, -, =, @, #, or $. Ordinals (1st, 2nd, 3rd etc.) and other combinations of numbers and letters are recognized as labels. Sometimes you may want to use a number, such as a year, as a label; in this case, you can type an apostrophe (') before it to make Excel recognize it as a label and disregard it when performing calculations. The apostrophe will not be visible in the cell, but will be shown in the formula bar when the cell is selected.

Figure 2-6 Entering values into the worksheet

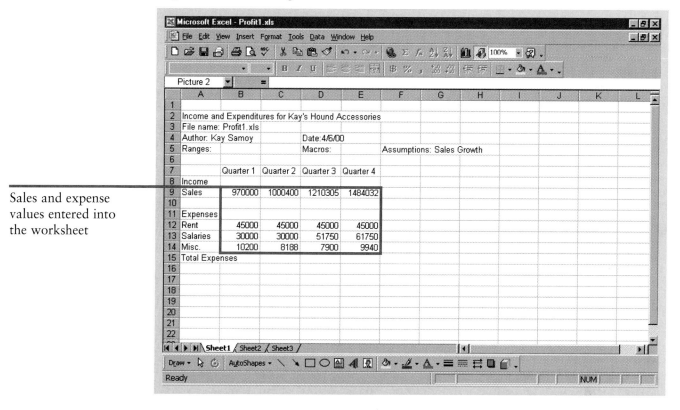

Sales and expense values entered into the worksheet

Excel 2000

Entering Formulas

Concept

Formulas allow Excel to perform calculations such as averages, sums, or products using values that have been entered into the worksheet.

Do It!

Kay would like to calculate the total expenses and profits for each quarter.

1 Click cell **B15** to activate it. This is the cell where the formula will be entered, and where the calculated result will appear.

2 Enter the following formula into the active cell: =B12+B13+B14. Notice that part of the label Total Expenses in cell A15 disappeared. You will learn how to widen columns in Lesson 3. The equals sign preceding the cell addresses and arithmetical operators prompts Excel to recognize the information as a formula. This calculation will result in a sum of the values in the three cells referenced in the formula.

3 Click the Enter button. The result, 85200, takes the place of the formula you entered in cell B15, and the formula remains visible in the formula bar, as shown in **Figure 2-7**.

4 Repeat steps 1-3 to enter similar formulas into cells C15, D15 and E15, substituting C, D, and E respectively for the Bs used above in the formula's cell addresses.

5 Click cell **A17** to activate it and enter the label Profit into the cell. Profit is the result of Income, or Sales, minus Total Expenses.

6 Click cell **B17** and enter the formula =B9-B15 into the cell, then press [Tab]. Excel subtracts First Quarter Expenses from First Quarter Sales to arrive at 884800, the profit for the First Quarter.

7 Repeat the previous step to enter similar formulas into cells C17, D17 and E17, substituting C, D, and E respectively for the Bs used above in the formula's cell addresses. Your worksheet should now resemble the one shown in **Figure 2-8**.

8 Save your workbook.

More

As you have seen, Excel formulas use cell addresses and the arithmetical operators; + for addition and – for subtraction. Since the standard computer keyboard does not contain multiplication or division symbols, the asterisk (*) is used for multiplication, and the forward slash (/) is used for division to specify the desired calculation. Using cell addresses, called cell referencing, helps Excel keep your calculations accurate by automatically recalculating results whenever the value in a cell referenced in a formula is altered.

Figure 2-7 Entering a formula

Formula displayed in
the formula bar

Results calculated using
the entered formula

Label in A15
partially covered

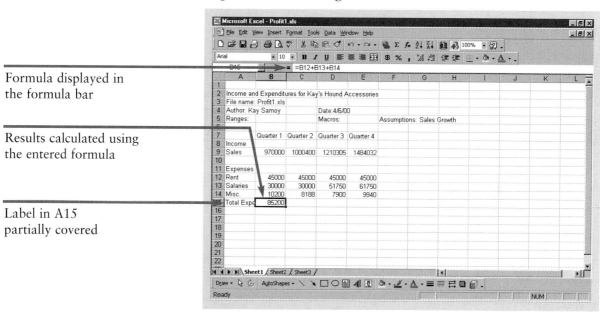

Excel 2000

Figure 2-8 Calculating Total Expenses and Profit

Results calculated in cells
containing formulas

New label entered into
cell A17

To practice entering formulas, follow the
instructions on the **Prac2-3** tab of the practice file **MyPractice 2.xls**.

Hot Tip

If you select two or more cells that contain
values, their sum will appear in the status
bar. Right-clicking the sum in the status bar
will open a pop-up menu that allows you
to select other forms of tabulation.

Using Functions

Concept

Instead of having to create a new formula each time you wish to perform a simple calculation in a worksheet, you can use one of Excel's predefined formulas, called **functions**. Excel has hundreds of these built-in formulas, covering many of the most common types of calculations performed by spreadsheets.

Do It!

Kay wants to use the SUM function to calculate her Total Expenses.

1 Click cell B15 to make it active.

2 Press [Delete] to clear the previously entered formula. The data disappears allowing the contents of cell A15 to be visible.

3 Click the **AutoSum** button Σ. The AutoSum function automatically sets up the formula for adding together the values directly above the active cell. The sum formula (=SUM B12:B14) appears in cell B15 and in the formula bar. The cells being added, called the argument, are indicated with an animated border (**Figure 2-9**). The sum formula contains the notation B12:B14, called a range, which refers to all cells between B12 and B14.

4 Press [Enter] to confirm Excel's assumption and apply the formula to the worksheet. The value 85200 appears in the cell.

5 Click cell F7, then enter the label **Total for Year**.

6 Click cell F9 to make it the active cell.

7 Click the **AutoSum** button Σ. The SUM function appears in the cell followed by the correct range B9:E9. Since there are no values above the active cell, AutoSum uses the values in the cells to the left of the cell pointer.

8 Click the **Enter** button. The value 4664737 now appears in the cell, as shown in **Figure 2-10**.

9 Save your worksheet.

More

In the example above, you used the AutoSum button to enter the SUM function into Cell B15 in place of the formula =B9+C9+D9+E9. But, unlike AutoSum, most Excel functions require the user to manually enter additional information after the function name. This information, enclosed in parentheses and called the **argument**, can be cell references or other data which the function needs to produce a result. The function acts upon the argument, as the SUM function above acted on the range of cells enclosed in the parentheses that followed it.

Figure 2-9 Using the AutoSum function

6					
7		Quarter 1	Quarter 2	Quarter 3	Quarter 4
8	Income				
9	Sales	970000	1000400	1210305	1484032
10					
11	Expenses				
12	Rent	45000	45000	45000	45000
13	Salaries	30000	30000	51750	61750
14	Misc.	10200	8188	7900	9940
15	Total Expe	=SUM(B12:B14)		104650	116690
16					
17	Profit	970000	917212	1105655	1367342
18					

Animated border indicating the argument of the formula

SUM formula

Excel 2000

Figure 2-10 Calculating the total expenses for the year

AutoSum button

SUM formula displayed in the formula bar

New label in cell F7

Total income for the year calculated in cell F9 using the AutoSum function

---

Practice

To practice using functions, follow the instructions on the **Prac2-4** tab of the practice file **MyPractice 2.xls**.

Hot Tip

Any range of cells may be selected as the argument for an AutoSum. Click the cell in which you wish the result to appear, click the AutoSum button, then select a new argument for the function by clicking and dragging over the desired range.

Using the Paste Function Feature

Concept

To enter a function other than SUM, you can either enter it yourself or use the Paste Function command. The Paste Function command allows you to insert built-in formulas into your worksheet, saving you the trouble of remembering mathematical expressions and the time it takes to type them.

Do It!

Kay would like to use the Paste Function command to calculate the average total quarterly expenses for the year.

1 Click cell B19 to activate it.

2 Click Insert, then click Function. The Paste Function dialog box will open (see Figure 2-11), and an equals sign will appear in the selected cell indicating that a formula is to follow.

3 Click Average in the Function name box to select it. A description of what the Average function does will appear below the function category and name boxes.

4 Click OK. The Paste Function dialog box will disappear, and the Formula Palette will appear with the range B17:B18 listed as the argument in the Number1 text box. Since this is not the correct range of cells, a new range must be specified as the argument.

5 To select the range for the total expenses, click cell B15, then drag to cell E15. An animated border will appear around the selected cells, and as you drag, the Edit Formula dialog box will reduce itself to the Number1 text box displaying the selected range. When you release the mouse button, the Formula Palette will reappear in full and the formula =AVERAGE (B15:E15) will appear in the formula bar and in cell B19, as shown in Figure 2-12.

6 Click OK. The Formula Palette closes and cell B19 will display the result 97432.

7 Click cell A19, then label it Ave. Exp. Your worksheet should now resemble the one shown in Figure 2-13.

8 Save your worksheet.

More

When the Paste Function dialog box appears, the default setting for the function category is Most Recently Used. If you have not used the Paste Function command before, this category contains a default list of commonly used functions. Each function on this list can also be found under a more specific category. To find other functions, you can select other categories by clicking on them. The list of Function Names changes to correspond to the category you have chosen.

You may have noticed that the title of the upper text box on the Formula Palette, Number1, is in bold face whereas the title of the text box beneath it is not. The bold title indicates that data must be entered in the box in order for the function to work. Plain text indicates that entering text is optional.

Figure 2-11 Paste Function dialog box

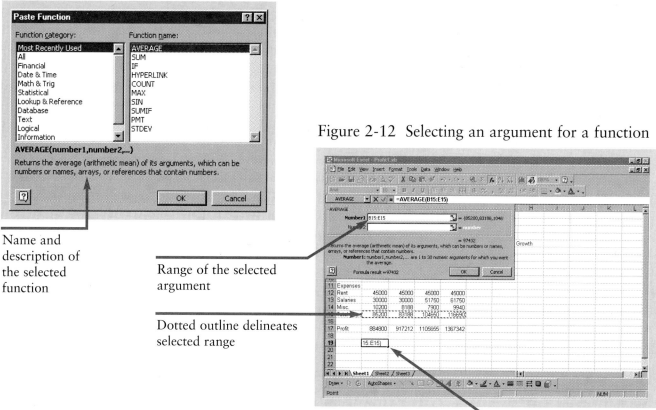

Name and
description of
the selected
function

Figure 2-12 Selecting an argument for a function

Range of the selected
argument

Dotted outline delineates
selected range

Formula is entered into
the active cell with the
selected range inserted
as the argument

Figure 2-13 Pasted function

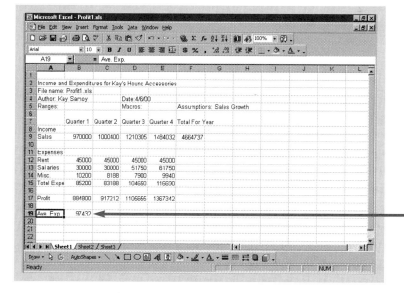

Result of the pasted function

Copying and Pasting Formulas

Concept

Formulas can be copied and pasted into other cells just like values or labels. Unless instructed otherwise, Excel considers the cell referred to in an argument to be a relative cell address. This means that if you copy a formula or function into another cell, Excel will substitute new cell references that are in the same position relative to the new formula or function location.

Do It!

To calculate the annual totals for her various expenses, Kay will copy the SUM function from cell F9 and paste it into cells F12, F13, F14, and F15.

1 Click cell F9 to activate it. The SUM function appears in the formula bar with the argument B9:E9.

2 Click the Copy button to copy the formula to the Windows Clipboard. An animated border appears around cell F9.

3 Click cell F12 to select it.

4 Click the Paste button to insert the copied function into the active cell. The result 180000 appears in cell F12. Notice that Excel has changed the argument in the formula bar from B9:F9 to B12:E12, the range of cell addresses relative to the copied function's position in the worksheet, so that the function will be applied to the row it is in rather than the one it was copied from.

5 Click the fill handle of the cell pointer surrounding cell F12 and drag down to cell F15. A gray border, shown in **Figure 2-14**, will appear around the range as you drag to indicate the target cells.

6 Release the mouse button. The SUM formula will be copied into cells F13, F14, and F15. Check your results against those in **Figure 2-15**.

7 Save the workbook as Profit1.xls.

More

Using relative cell references is similar to giving directions that explain where to go from the present location. Relative cell references follow the same directional instructions regardless of your starting position, such as "the four cells to the left of" or "the three cells above." In the preceding example, the formula told Excel to calculate the average of the values in the four cells to the left of the cell containing the formula. Wherever that formula is pasted, Excel will examine the four cells to the left of the target cell for values. Any cells that are blank, or do not contain values (such as those with labels), will be included in the calculation as zero. If you had attempted to paste the AVERAGE formula used above into a cell in column B, there would not be enough cells to the left of the target cell to fulfill the required argument, and the error message #REF! would have appeared in the cell.

Figure 2-14 Copying a formula using the fill handle

Formula will be pasted into these cells when the fill handle is released

Figure 2-15 Results of copied formula

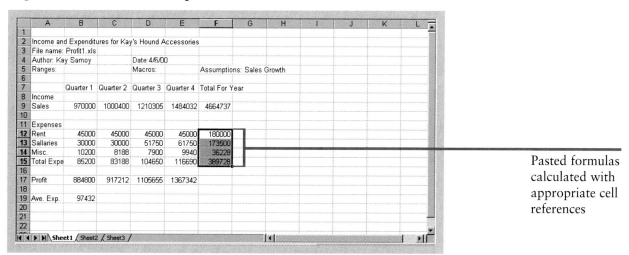

Pasted formulas calculated with appropriate cell references

Practice

To practice copying and pasting formulas, follow the instructions on the **Prac2-6** tab of the practice file **MyPractice 2.xls**.

Hot Tip

You can select which characteristics of a cell's data you wish to paste by using the **Paste Special** command on the Edit menu.

Using What-If Analysis

Concept

Excel makes it easy for you to change certain conditions in your worksheet, allowing you to see how these changes affect the results of various spreadsheet calculations. This is called **What-If analysis**, and is one of Excel's most useful features. It can be used to produce hypothetical and true projections of your data. Businesses benefit from this type of analysis because they can gain insight into the future with it and act accordingly.

Do It!

Kay wants to see what her sales would have been in Quarters 2, 3, and 4, assuming they grew 10% from the amount shown for the first quarter ($970,000).

1 Select the contents of cells C9, D9, and E9. These are the sales figures for the second, third, and fourth quarters and will be recalculated with the new assumption.

2 Press [Delete] to remove the values from the selected cells. Notice that the values in cells F9 and C15:E15 change. This is due to the fact that Excel automatically recalculates formulas when values in their referenced cells have been altered. The values in cells C9:E9 are now considered to be zero.

3 Click cell I5 to select it.

4 Enter .1 (10% expressed as a decimal) into the active cell. This is the cell that will be referenced in the formula that calculates projected earnings.

5 Click cell C9 to select it. Notice that Excel inserts a zero before the .1 in cell I5 as a place holder.

6 Now you must create a formula to multiply first quarter sales by 110%, which will show the results of a 10% increase. Enter the formula =B9*(1+I5) into the active cell, as shown in **Figure 2-16**. The dollar signs preceding the column letter I and the row number 5 tell Excel not to change the cell address, even if the formula is moved to a new location. This is known as an **absolute cell reference**.

7 Press [Enter]. The result of the calculation, 1067000, appears in place of the formula in cell C9. Cell F9 and B17 both change to reflect Excel's recalculation of their formulas, which include the cell C9 in their argument.

Figure 2-16 Using absolute cell references to perform What-If analysis

B9 is a relative cell address, while I5 represents an absolute cell address

The formula in the active cell will refer to this cell even if it is copied elsewhere

Using What-If Analysis (continued)

Do It!

8 Click the Copy button 📋 to copy the cell's formula to the Clipboard. A animated border appears around cell C9 to indicate that the selection is ready to be copied.

9 Click cell **D9** to activate it, then click the **Paste** button 📋. The pasted formula appears in the formula bar and the result, 1173700, appears in the cell. Notice that the reference to cell B9 has changed to C9, but that the reference to cell I5 remains the same. If the dollar signs had not been included, the copied formula would have replaced the cell reference I5 with J5, an empty cell, and the result would have been wrong.

10 Click cell **E9** to activate it, then click the **Paste** button 📋. As before, the formula is pasted and a new result, 1291070, appears in the cell, as shown in **Figure 2-17**.

11 Press [Enter] to confirm that the correct formula has been pasted into the target cell.

12 Click the Save button 💾 to save your work.

More

Formulas can contain several **operations**. An operation is a single mathematical step in solving an equation, such as adding two numbers or calculating an exponent. When working with formulas that contain multiple operators, such as 12/200+4*8, Excel performs the calculations in the following order:

1. Parentheses
2. Exponents
3. Multiplication and division, from left to right
4. Addition and subtraction, from left to right

Operations inside parentheses are calculated first, in accordance with the rules above. For example, in the calculation 12/200+4*8, the operations would be performed as follows: first, 12 would be divided by 200, then four would be multiplied by 8, and finally the two results would be added together. If the equation was 12/(200+4)*8, then the operations would be calculated like this: first, 200 would be added to 4, then 12 would be divided by the result, and finally the dividend would be multiplied by 8.

Figure 2-17 Copying a formula containing an absolute cell address

Though the relative cell address changed from B9 to D9 when the formula was copied, the absolute address for cell I5 remains unchanged

Practice

To practice using absolute cell references and What-If analysis, follow the instructions on the **Prac2-7** tab of the practice file **MyPractice 2.xls**.

Hot Tip

If you want both the column and row in a cell reference to remain absolute, then a $ must be placed in front of each. Placing a $ before only one part of the reference will make only that part absolute, while the other remains relative.

EX 2.19

Previewing and Printing a Worksheet

Concept

Printing your worksheet is useful if you would like to have a paper copy to file, reference, or distribute to others. While offices are becoming more and more electronic, many people still prefer working with paper documents to viewing them on a screen. Excel allows you to view the worksheet as it will appear on the printed page before it is printed so that you can spot errors or items you would like to change before going through the printing process.

Do It!

Kay will display her worksheet in Print Preview mode, then print it.

1 Make sure your computer is properly connected to a working printer. (Ask your instructor.)

2 Click the Print Preview button ⬜ on the Standard toolbar. The worksheet will be displayed in Print Preview mode, as shown in **Figure 2-18**. The mouse pointer appears as a magnifying glass 🔍.

3 Click at the top of the preview page. The worksheet will be magnified so that you may examine it more closely, and the pointer will change to an arrow. Since gridlines are nonprinting items, they do not appear in the preview.

4 Click Print... on the Print Preview toolbar. The view will revert to regular mode and the Print dialog box, **Figure 2-19**, will open.

5 Click OK. The Print dialog box will close, a box will appear notifying you of the print job's progress, and the document will be sent to the printer.

More

You can adjust many printing options by selecting the Page Setup command on the File menu. The Page Setup dialog box will open with four tabs; Page, Margins, Header/Footer, and Sheet. The Page tab controls the way in which the printed selection will appear on the page, such as its horizontal or vertical orientation, or by how much or little it is magnified. The Margins tab allows you to adjust the amount of space between printed matter and the edges of the page. The Header/Footer tab allows you to enter items that will appear at the top or bottom of each page, such as page numbers, titles, file names, or the name of the author. The Sheet tab lets you select how your data is presented on the printed page, such as whether or not you want to print gridlines, which parts of the worksheet you wish to print, and whether you want column headings to be repeated across each new page.

Figure 2-18 Previewing you worksheet

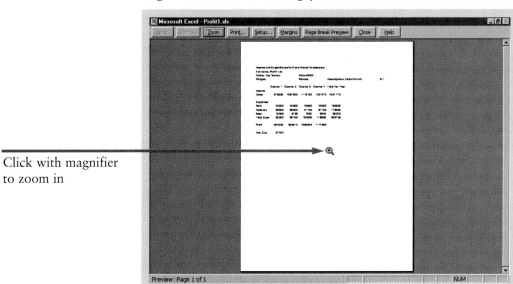

Click with magnifier
to zoom in

Figure 2-19 Print dialog box

Name of the
selected printer

Click arrow buttons
or enter a number to
change the number
of copies that will be
printed

Specifies that all of
the current worksheet
will be printed

To practice previewing and printing worksheets, follow the instructions on the
Prac2-8 tab of the practice file **MyPractice
2.xls**.

Hot Tip

If you do not need to conduct a print
preview or adjust the settings in the Print
dialog box, you can print the active worksheet by clicking the Print button 🖨 on
the Standard toolbar.

Function	Button/Mouse	Menu	Keyboard
Copy data to the Clipboard		Click Edit, then click Copy	[Ctrl]+[C]
Cut data to the Clipboard		Click Edit, then click Cut	[Ctrl]+[X]
Paste data from the Clipboard		Click Edit, then click Paste	[Ctrl]+[V]
AutoSum			
Paste Function		Click Insert, then click Function	
Print Preview		Click File, then click Print Preview	
Print	(to skip Print dialog box)	Click File, then click Print (for Print dialog box)	[Ctrl]+[P] (for Print dialog box)

Identify Key Features

Name the items indicated by callouts in **Figure 2-20**.

Figure 2-20 Features of an Excel screen and worksheet

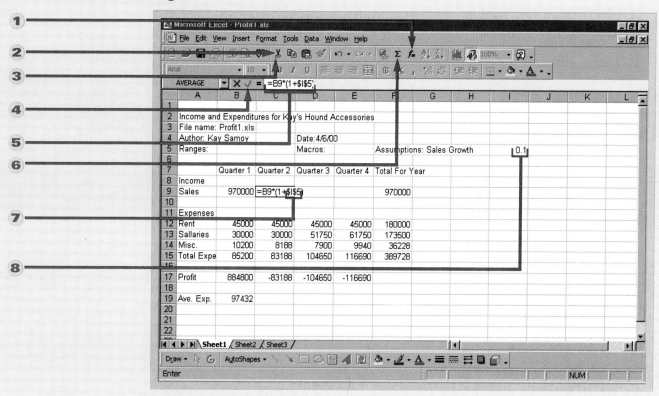

Select The Best Answer

9. The small square in the lower-right corner of the active cell

10. A temporary storage space for cut or copied information

11. Use this symbol to represent multiplication in a formula

12. Allows you to view a worksheet as it will appear on an actual page

13. Lets you adjust margins or switch the page orientation

14. Offers AVERAGE as one of its choices

15. Aligned to the right by default

16. Type this symbol to designate a cell reference as absolute

a. Page Setup dialog box

b. Print Preview

c. Paste Function dialog box

d. Dollar sign

e. Fill handle

f. Clipboard

g. Asterisk

h. Values

Quiz (continued)

Complete the Statement

17. When using the fill handle, cells to be filled are indicated by a:

    a. ScreenTip

    b. Plus sign

    c. Check mark

    d. Gray border

18. Typing an apostrophe before a number instructs Excel to recognize it as a:

    a. Label

    b. Value

    c. Function

    d. Formula

19. All of the following actions will erase the Clipboard except:

    a. Pasting an item

    b. Cutting a new item

    c. Copying a new item

    d. Turning off the computer

20. By default, Excel considers referenced cell addresses to be:

    a. Absolute

    b. Copied from the Clipboard

    c. Relative

    d. AutoSums

21. Changing conditions to see how the results affect spreadsheet calculations is called:

    a. Absolute analysis

    b. Variable analysis

    c. Assumption analysis

    d. What-If analysis

22. To copy cell contents to a new location, drag-and-drop the cell pointer while pressing:

    a. [Shift]

    b. [Enter]

    c. [Tab]

    d. [Ctrl]

23. An animated border indicates that the cell contents:

    a. Will be deleted

    b. Are the result of a function or formula

    c. Have been sent to the Clipboard

    d. Have been pasted

24. The information enclosed in parentheses in a function is called the:

    a. Quantifier

    b. Argument

    c. Cell reference

    d. AutoSum

Interactivity

Test Your Skills

1. Enter values into your spreadsheet:

   a. Open the file you created in the first lesson, Test 1.xls.

   b. Fill in values to display how many hours you spend on each activity every day. For example, if you have four hours of class on Monday, enter the number 4 in the cell where the Monday column intersects with the Class row.

   c. If any of the values are repeated during the week, use the copy and paste commands to copy them from one cell to the others.

2. Use the AutoSum function to total the number of hours you spend on each activity during the week.

   a. Create a Total Hours label in the same row as the days of the week labels, in the column directly to the right of the Sunday column.

   b. Use AutoSum to enter the total hours you spend in Class in the cell where the Total Hours column and the Class row intersect.

   c. Use the fill handle to copy the AutoSum function into the next five cells in the Total Hours column in order to calculate the Total Hours for the remaining daily activities.

3. Calculate the average time you spend on each activity each week by using the Paste Function command:

   a. Enter the label Average in the cell directly to the right of Total Hours.

   b. Select the cell where the Average column intersects with the Class row. Then use the Paste Function command to place the average number of hours spent in class during the week in the active cell.

   c. Place the averages for the five other daily activities in the Average column by using the fill handle.

4. Preview and print the worksheet:

   a. Switch to Print Preview mode.

   b. Zoom in on the right side of the worksheet.

   c. Change the orientation of the page to Landscape.

   d. Print the worksheet.

   e. Return to normal view and save the file as Test 2.xls.

Excel 2000

Interactivity (continued)

Problem Solving

1. Using the skills you have learned so far, create a spreadsheet that will allow you to track your individual monthly expenses for a year. Divide the year into four quarters, and use category labels such as rent, phone bill, books or supplies, food, entertainment, etc. Calculate your total expenses for each quarter, as well as your average quarterly expenses. Also include an assumption value of five percent to account for going over your allotted budget. Then conduct a What-If analysis to recalculate your total and average expenses based on a five percent increase in one of the categories. Save the file as Solved 2.xls.

2. Open the file Solved-HR.xls, which you created at the end of Lesson 1. To review, you designed this spreadsheet to detail how you will use the $10,000 dollar increase in your Human Resources expense account to improve recruiting. Now it is time to put the spreadsheet to work. Enter values to fill in the existing structure. Then add a label for a cell in which you can add up the different monetary allotments to demonstrate that you have not surpassed the $10,000 amount. Use a formula or function to calculate this total. Print a copy of the file, and then save the it as Solved-HR2.xls.

3. Open the file Solved-Rest.xls, which you also created in Lesson 1. Using fictional names and hours, complete the weekly waitstaff schedule that you designed. If your worksheet does not already have one, include a column that will store the total hours for each staff member each day, one for total hours for the week, and one for average hours per day. Using the skills you learned in this lesson, instruct Excel to calculate the data for these columns. When you have finished, print the worksheet and save it as Solved-Rest2.xls.

L E S S O N

3

FORMATTING WORKSHEET ELEMENTS

As you work with your spreadsheet, you will find that you use certain groups of cells that contain related data repeatedly. Excel allows you to define these groups as ranges, and name them as you see fit. Then, rather then select the range by dragging the mouse over it, you can select the appropriate cells quickly and accurately with the name box.

Formatting refers to changing the appearance of information in a worksheet without changing its actual content. You can use Excel's many formatting tools to improve the appearance and the effectiveness of your spreadsheet. Text formatting includes font, font size, style, color, and alignment. Labels can also be formatted in a variety of styles, some of which help to express the kind of data they represent. You can format individual cells or ranges of cells. The AutoFormat command permits you to apply a set of predesigned formats to an entire range at once.

Although the structure of an Excel spreadsheet is highly organized, it is also very flexible. You can change the structure by increasing or decreasing column widths and row heights. You can also add and delete rows and columns as necessary. Changes to the structure of your worksheet depend on the data it contains and the formatting you have applied.

CASE STUDY
Kay will continue to develop and organize her spreadsheet by naming her ranges and adding formatting to her data. She will also modify the physical structure of the worksheet in order to improve its layout.

Defining and Naming Ranges

Concept

A range is any group of two or more cells, usually contiguous. The range B12 to E12 consists of these two cells, called anchor cells, and all cells between them. The data for this range is Kay's rent. Range addresses are defined by citing the first and last cell in the range separated by a colon. The address for the range for Kay's rent is B12:E12. Ranges are named so that they are easy to locate. These names can also be used in formulas. You can name a range using the Name Box or the Define Name dialog box.

Do It!

Kay wants to define and name all of the ranges in her worksheet that contain data.

1. Click cell B9, then drag to cell F9 to select these cells. The range for Sales is defined as B9:F9, and will be highlighted.

2. Click the inside the Name Box [B9 ▾]. The cell name B9 will become active, indicated by its highlighting.

3. Type Sales, then press [Enter]. The range B9:F9 is now named Sales, and the range name will appear in the Name Box whenever cells B9 to F9 are selected.

4. Repeat this process to name the remaining row labels, being sure to press [Enter] after each range name. Name the range B12:E12 Rent, the range B13:E13 Salaries, the range B14:E14 Miscellaneous, the range B15:E15 Total_Expenses, and range B17:E17 Profit. Be sure to include the underscore ([Shift]+[-]) in the name Total_Expenses, as range names cannot contain any spaces. When you click the Name box drop-down arrow your Name Box list should now resemble the one shown in **Figure 3-1**.

Figure 3-1 Defining and naming ranges

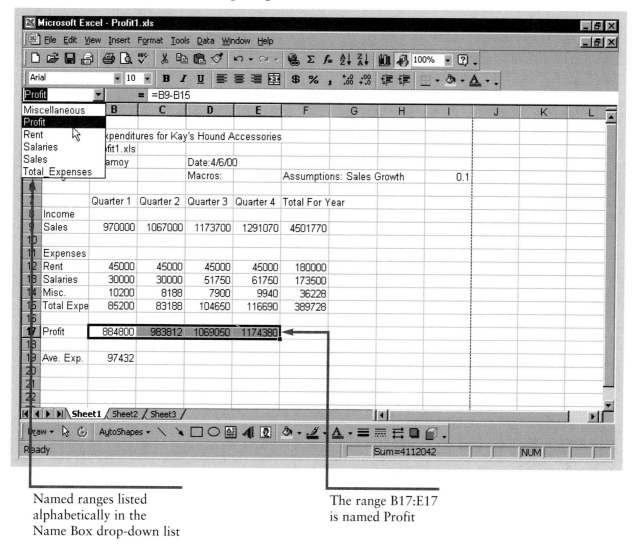

Named ranges listed
alphabetically in the
Name Box drop-down list

The range B17:E17
is named Profit

Defining and Naming Ranges (continued)

Do It!

5 Click cell B8, and drag down to cell B17. The range B8:B17 will be selected.

6 Click Insert, highlight Name, then click Define. The Define Name dialog box, shown in **Figure 3-2**, will open with the range name Quarter_1 in the Names in Workbook text box. Excel automatically picks up a column or row label as the default range name if it is adjacent to, or included in, the range selected. You can change this name if you wish, but we will use the defaults for this exercise.

7 Click [OK] to name the range.

8 Click cell C8, then hold [Shift] down and click cell C17. The range C8:C17 will become highlighted. Holding the shift key down highlights all of the cells between the first and the last cells you select.

9 Repeat step six to name this range Quarter_2.

10 Use the Define Name dialog box to name the range D8:D17 Quarter_3, the range E8:E17 Quarter_4, and the range F8:F17 Total_for_Year.

11 Click elsewhere in the worksheet to deselect the range.

12 Click the Save button 🖫 to save the changes you have made to the worksheet.

More

Ranges do not have to be made up of cells that are touching. They can contain nonadjacent blocks of cells, or multiple nonadjoining cells. To create a nonadjacent range, highlight the first group of cells or a single cell that you wish to include, then hold down [Ctrl] while selecting the next cluster of cells. You can select as many noncontiguous cells or ranges as you desire. Clicking anywhere else in the worksheet will deselect the ranges.

Figure 3-2 Define Name dialog box

Label above selected range is used as default range name

List of named ranges

Click to delete a selected range

Practice

Open the practice file **Practice-Lesson 3.xls**, save it as **MyPractice3,** and then follow the instructions on the **Prac3-1** tab.

Hot Tip

Use the Name Box drop-down list to quickly select a range to be used in a formula or to be formatted.

Formatting Cell Contents

Concept

Formatting enhances the appearance of your worksheet and can make your labels stand out, so they will be easier to read. Formatting options include changing the font (typeface and size), style, and alignment of your text. A cell or range must be selected before formatting can be applied to it.

Do It!

Kay wants to add formatting to various cells to emphasize their contribution to the worksheet.

1 Click the Name box drop down arrow, then click Profit on the list of named ranges that appears. If Profit had not been visible, you would have had to use the scroll bar on the right edge of the list to access the rest of the range names it contains.

2 Click Format, then click Cells. The Format Cells dialog box will open.

3 Click the Font tab to bring it to the front of the stack, as shown in **Figure 3-3**.

4 Notice that the current font (Arial), font style (regular), and size (10 point) are highlighted. From the Font Style list, select Bold. The letters in the Preview box will be made bold so that you may view the results of this change before you apply it.

5 Click OK. The dialog box will close and the numbers contained in the range named Profit will appear bold, as shown in **Figure 3-4**.

6 Click cell A2 to make it active.

7 Click the Font box drop-down arrow. A list of the fonts installed on your computer will appear.

8 Drag the scroll bar box on the Font list down until Times New Roman is visible, then move the pointer over Times New Roman and click. The typeface of "Income and Expenditures for Kay's Hound Accessories" will change from Arial to Times New Roman.

9 Click the Font Size text box. The current point size of 10 will become highlighted, ready to be changed.

10 Type 14, then press [Enter]. The title will increase in size.

11 Select the range A2:K2. These are the columns across which the title will be centered.

12 Click the Merge and Center button ▦, then click elsewhere on the worksheet to deselect the columns. **Figure 3-5** shows the new title placement.

Figure 3-3 Format Cells dialog box

Current font, font style, and size are highlighted

Preview area displays how the selected font will appear with the chosen attributes

Figure 3-4 Bolding cell data

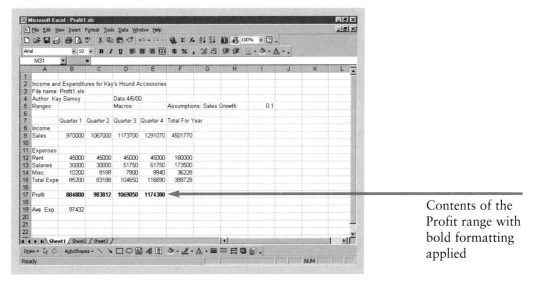

Contents of the Profit range with bold formatting applied

Figure 3-6 Formatted worksheet title

Font Size text box

Font box drop-down arrow

Worksheet title in 14 point, Times New Roman and centered across cells A through K

Formatting Cell Contents (continued)

Do It!

13 Select the range B7:F7.

14 Click the Italic button $\boxed{I}$. The column labels will change to italicized type.

15 Click the Underline button $\boxed{U}$. Each column label will be underlined. Notice that the Italic and Underline buttons are indented. An indented button indicates that a particular formatting option is being applied.

16 Select the range A8:A19.

17 Click the right edge, the arrow, of the Font Color button $\boxed{A}$. The Font Color palette, shown in **Figure 3-6**, will open.

18 Select the blue color box in the second row of the palette, then click anywhere on the worksheet to deselect the range. The row labels will change to blue. Your worksheet should appear as the one shown in **Figure 3-7**.

19 Click File, then click Save to save your work.

More

The Font tab in the Format Cells dialog box allows you to change most of the attributes relating to text. The options Font, Font style, and Size each have two boxes attached to them. The lower box is a list box that indexes available fonts, font styles, and font sizes respectively. The upper box is a text box wherein you can enter any of these choices without having to scroll through the list. However, the point size of your font selection is not limited to only those numbers listed, and can be anywhere between 1 and 409.

The Underline option contains a drop-down list with five styles of underlines that can be used. The Color option contains a drop-down palette with 56 color choices. Clicking one of these boxes will turn your text that color. Checking the Normal Font box reverts any changed font formats to the default settings described above. There are three effects you can select: Strikethrough draws a line through text, making it appear as if it has been crossed out; Superscript shrinks the text and raises it above the baseline; Subscript shrinks and drops the text below the baseline. Any alteration to a font formatting characteristic that you make will appear in the preview window in the tab, and none of the changes made will take effect on the worksheet until the OK button is clicked.

Figure 3-6 Font Color palette

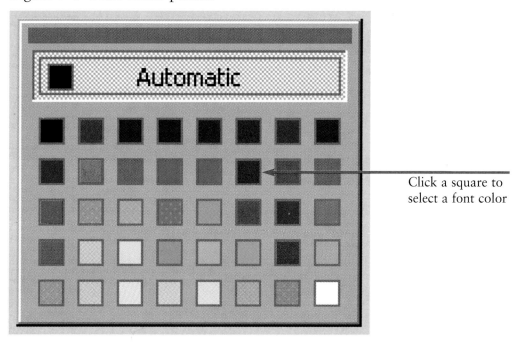

Click a square to
select a font color

Figure 3-7 Formatted cell contents

Italicized and underlined
cell labels

Cell labels with
color applied

To practice formatting cell labels, follow the
instructions on the **Prac3-2** tab of the practice file **MyPractice3.xls**.

Hot Tip

Clicking an indented formatting button
removes the applied format and reverts the
button to its normal, flat, state.

Working with Rows and Columns

Concept

There are times when the information you enter into your worksheet will not fit neatly into a cell set with the default height and width. Therefore you may need to adjust the height of a row or, more commonly, the width of a column. The standard column width is 8.43 characters, but can be set anywhere between 0 and 255.

Do It!

Kay wants to widen some of the columns in her worksheet to accommodate long labels and values.

1 Move the mouse pointer onto the dividing line between the column A and column B heading buttons. The pointer will change from a cross ✚ to a double-arrow ◄► that will allow you to resize the column.

2 Click and hold the left mouse button. The gridline that divides the columns will become dotted and the column width will appear in a ScreenTip.

3 With the mouse button depressed, drag the column boundary to the right until the width reaches 13.00 characters. The entire label "Total Expenses" will be visible. While the "Total Expenses" label was cropped before you resized the column, notice that the label in cell F7, Total for Year, is fully visible. Excel will display a label that is longer than its cell is wide in its entirety as long as the cell it intrudes upon is empty.

4 Click the column B heading button to select the entire column.

5 While holding [Ctrl], click the column C, D, E, and F heading buttons so that all five columns are selected, as shown in **Figure 3-8**.

6 Click Format, highlight Column, then select Width from the submenu. The Column Width dialog box, **Figure 3-9**, will open.

7 Type 14 in the Column Width text box, then click ⎡ OK ⎤. Columns B through F will increase in width to 14 characters. This width is to accommodate formatting that you will apply to the cell data in a later skill.

8 Save your work.

More

You can also adjust the height of the rows in your worksheet. Row height is measured in points, just as fonts are, and there are 72 points per inch. Dragging the line between two row heading buttons is one way to change a row's height. There is a Row command on the Format menu that allows you to alter height as well. Row height usually does not need to be changed manually, as Excel will adjust row height to fit the largest point size of a cell's label or data.

Table 3-1 Column formatting commands

COMMAND	FUNCTION
Width	Adjust the width to a specified number of characters
AutoFit Selection	Adjust the width to fit the widest cell entry
Hide	Hides a selected column from view
Unhide	Displays a hidden column
Standard Width	Allows you to set a default width size, and resets selected columns to the specified size

Excel 2000

Figure 3-8 Selecting columns to be resized

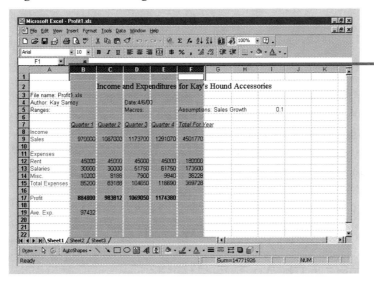

Columns B through F selected

Figure 3-9 Column Width dialog box

Practice

To practice working with column and row widths, follow the instructions on the **Prac3-3** tab of the practice file **MyPractice3.xls**.

Hot Tip

You can resize a column's width to fit the widest entry automatically by double-clicking the right edge of the column heading button.

Inserting and Deleting Rows and Columns

Concept

In Excel you can add and delete columns or rows to customize your worksheet to your specific needs. For example, you may want to add another column for new inventory products, or perhaps even delete a row that contains expenses that are no longer current.

Do It!

Kay wants to add an additional row between her documentation sections and the main body of her worksheet, and she wants to remove the column between Assumptions and the assumption value.

1 Click cell **A6** to make it active.

2 Click **Insert**, then click the **Cells** command. The Insert dialog box, **Figure 3-10**, will open with the **Shift cells down** radio button selected.

3 Click the **Entire Row** radio button. This tells Excel to add a row and shift all of the rows below row 6 down.

4 Click **OK**. A new row will be inserted, the contents of the worksheet will shift down by one row, and your formulas will be updated to reflect the row shift.

5 Click cell **H5** to make it active.

6 Click **Edit**, the click **Delete**. The Delete dialog box, similar to Insert, will open with the **Shift Cells Left** radio button selected.

7 Click the **Entire column** radio button, then click **OK**. Cell H5 will be deleted and the Sales Growth data will move from I5 to H5. Even though the Sales values for Quarters 2 through 4 are based on the absolute address of the assumption, Excel will recalculate the formulas based on the new cell address. Compare your worksheet with that of **Figure 3-11**.

8 Save your workbook.

More

A **dummy column** or **dummy row** is a blank column or row included at the end of a defined range that is used to hold a place or create blank space. A dummy row between a range of values and a cell containing a formula to average them allows Excel to include the added row in the range rather than considering it to be an unrelated value. Then, if a row or column is added to the original range, Excel will recalculate any formulas that include that range to include the change. If you need to add a row or column to a range that does not include a dummy, you must manually adjust your formulas to take into account the new cells and values. If a row or column is inserted into the middle of an existing range, Excel is able to recalculate any formulas that reference that range. It is only when you need to add a row or column to the end of an existing range that is being used in a formula that a dummy row or column becomes necessary.

Figure 3-10 Insert dialog box

Click here to insert an entire row, not
just a single cell, into your worksheet

Figure 3-11 Worksheet with a row inserted and a cell deleted

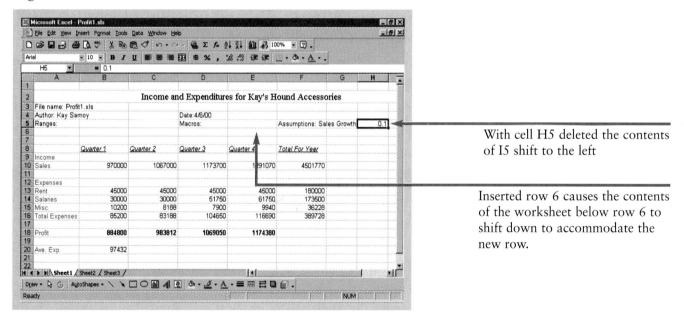

With cell H5 deleted the contents
of I5 shift to the left

Inserted row 6 causes the contents
of the worksheet below row 6 to
shift down to accommodate the
new row.

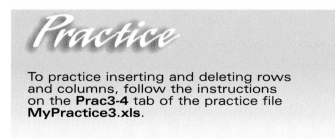

To practice inserting and deleting rows
and columns, follow the instructions
on the **Prac3-4** tab of the practice file
MyPractice3.xls.

Right-clicking (clicking the right mouse
button) brings up various pop-up menus.
Where you right-click in the Excel window
will determine which pop-up menu
appears. Try right-clicking various elements
of the Excel window to view these menus.

Formatting Cell Values

Concept

Although labels can help identify what kind of data a number represents, you may want to format the values themselves so that their function is more apparent. Common formats include Currency, Percentage, Fraction, and Comma. The format you choose will depend on how the values are to be used, and how you wish them to appear. Cell or range formatting can be applied before or after data is entered.

Do It!

Kay wants to format all of her values with commas so that they will be easier to read, format the Profit range in Currency Style, format her assumption in Percentage Style, and then decrease the number of decimal places in cell B20.

1 Select the range B10:F20.

2 Click the Comma Style button ⬚. All of the cells contained within the selected range will be formatted in the Comma Style, which includes two decimal places.

3 Click the Name Box drop down list arrow, then click Profit on the list of ranges that appears. The range B18:F18 will be highlighted.

4 Click the Currency Style button ⬚. The values entered in the Profit row will appear with dollar signs preceding them and two decimal places to represent cents.

5 Click cell H5 to make it the active cell.

6 Click the Percentage Style button ⬚. The originally entered value of 0.1 will appear as 10%. The result of the formula whose argument references this cell will remain the same.

7 Click cell B20 to activate it.

8 Click the Decrease Decimal button ⬚ twice. The two decimal places will be erased. **Figure 3-12** displays the worksheet as it should now appear.

9 Save the worksheet.

More

When you applied the Currency, Comma, and Percentage Styles to the worksheet, you used the default settings for each of these buttons. The Number tab of the Format Cells dialog box, shown in **Figure 3-13**, can be accessed by selecting the Cells command on the Format menu. It allows you to apply one of twelve different formatting styles to cells. Most of the categories of formatting listed on the Numbers tab can be customized to suit the specific needs of your worksheet and personal preferences.

The number of decimal place values taken and the appearance of date and time references can be altered, special formats can be defined for use in databases, and custom number formats can be created for advanced users of Excel.

Figure 3-12 Cell values with formatting applied

Percentage Style

Comma Style

Currency Style

Decimal places
reduced by two

Figure 3-13 Format Cells dialog box

Click a category to
select a formatting
style

Click a type to
choose how the
selected style
will appear

Practice

To practice formatting cell values, follow
the instructions on the **Prac3-5** tab of the
practice file **MyPractice3.xls**.

Hot Tip

If a cell is too narrow to display a value
correctly, Excel will display number signs
(######) in place of the data, though the
actual value is unaffected. Making the cell
wide enough to accommodate the data
properly will make it reappear correctly.

Using AutoFormat

Concept

The AutoFormat command allows you to add one of sixteen sets of formatting to selected ranges, creating tables that are easy to read and are visually stimulating. Numbers, borders, fonts, patterns, alignment, and the height and width of rows and columns can all be altered using the AutoFormat options. AutoFormat alters the appearance of tables using colors, fonts, and textures.

Do It!

Kay wants to use the AutoFormat function to improve the appearance of her worksheet and set the main body data off from the documentation.

1. Select the range A8:F20 to make this area active.

2. Click Format, then select the AutoFormat command. The AutoFormat dialog box, shown in **Figure 3-14** will open.

3. Drag the Table Format list box scroll bar down to reveal the lower portion of the Table Format list, then select 3D Effects 2.

4. Click [OK], then click anywhere in the worksheet to deselect the area. The range A8:F20 will appear as shown in **Figure 3-15**.

5. Select the range A3:H5 to make this group of cells active.

6. Click Format, then select AutoFormat to open the AutoFormat dialog box.

7. Select List 1 from the Table Format list, then click the Options button [Options >>]. The AutoFormat dialog box will grow to display six format types which you can include or exclude when the AutoFormat is applied.

8. Click Font, Width/Height, and Alignment so they do not display a check in their check boxes. The Sample table will show how the range will look with these options off. These options were turned off so as to preserve the font, size and placement of the title and the width of the columns.

9. Click [OK], then click anywhere in the worksheet to deselect the range. **Figure 3-16** shows the worksheet documentation with the AutoFormatting.

10. Save your workbook.

Figure 3-14   AutoFormat dialog box

Each AutoFormat style includes a customizable preview

Figure 3-15   AutoFormatting applied to the selected range

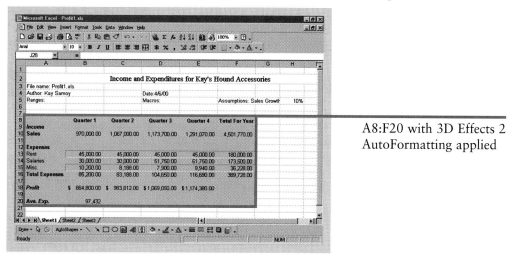

A8:F20 with 3D Effects 2 AutoFormatting applied

Figure 3-16   List 1 AutoFormatting applied

A3:H5 with List 1 AutoFormatting applied with Font, Width/Height, and Alignment left intact

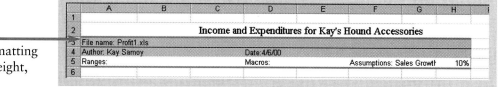

Practice

To practice using AutoFormat, follow the instructions on the **Prac3-6** tab of the practice file **MyPractice3.xls**.

Hot Tip

The None option on the Table Format list in the AutoFormat dialog box will return a range to its original, unformatted style.

Filling a Range with Labels

Concept

Excel can automatically fill a range with several types of series information. Series information includes numbers, numbers combined with text (such as Quarter 1), dates, and times. Excel can step, or increase, a series by a constant set value, or multiply by a constant factor. For example, you can add all the months of the year to a worksheet by typing only January and then extending the series. The way a series fills will depend on the type of value and the incremental setting.

Do It!

To practice the **AutoFill** feature, Kay will erase the Quarter column headings and then replace them with a series fill.

1 Click cell **B8** to select it, then press the [Back Space] key to delete the cell label.

2 Repeat this process for cells **C8**, **D8**, and **E8**. The range B8:E8 will be empty.

3 Click cell **B8**, then type **Quarter 1**.

4 Move the mouse pointer to the fill handle of the cell pointer surrounding cell **B8**. It will change to the crosshairs.

5 Drag the pointer to cell **E8** with the fill handle. As you drag the pointer, a dimmed border will appear indicating the cells that have been selected, and ScreenTips will appear showing what will be placed the cell where the mouse pointer currently is, as shown in **Figure 3-17**.

6 Release the mouse button. The range B8:E8 will be filled with Quarter 1 through Quarter 4.

7 Close your workbook without saving changes,

More

In the above example, you used **AutoFill** to enter a series of labels into a range of cells. Along with AutoFill, there are three other series fill types that you can use: Linear, Growth, and Date. These are advanced options and are found in the Series dialog box, shown in **Figure 3-18**, which can be accessed by clicking the Edit menu, selecting Fill, and then clicking Series on the submenu.

A Linear series fill, with the Trend box unchecked, adds the Step value to the value in the cell selected. With Trend checked, the Step value is disregarded and the trend is calculated based on the average of the difference between the values in the selected cells. This average is then used to fill the range by increasing or decreasing the value by a constant amount. If necessary, the original selected cell information is replaced to fit the trend.

A Growth series fill is similar to a Linear series fill, except that instead of adding values together, numbers are multiplied to create a geometric growth trend. A series created based upon dates uses the options in the Date Units list. You can extend selected dates by day, weekday, month, or year. The Stop value can be set so as to fix a value at which the series will end. If the selected range is filled before it reaches the Stop value, it will end at that point.

Figure 3-17 Filling a range with labels

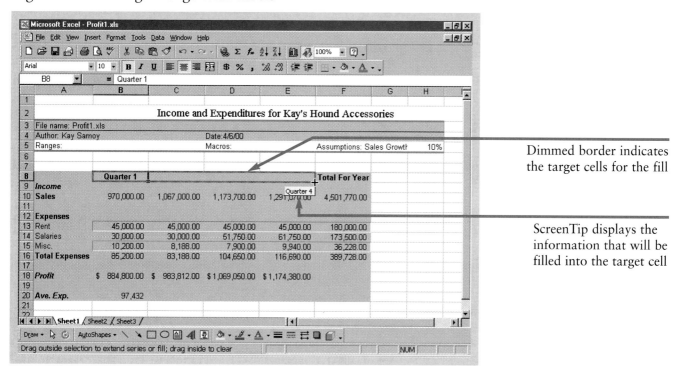

Dimmed border indicates
the target cells for the fill

ScreenTip displays the
information that will be
filled into the target cell

Excel 2000

Figure 3-18 Series dialog box

Practice

To practice filing ranges with labels follow
the instructions on the **Prac3-7** tab of the
practice file **MyPractice3.xls**.

Hot Tip

If you select a value, and then hold the
right mouse button while dragging the fill
handle, a pop-up menu will appear allowing
you to choose the type of series that is
inserted into the destination cells.

Formatting Cells and Ranges

Concept

As you have seen, you can format the contents of spreadsheet cells in order to make the spreadsheet more pleasing to the eye and more comprehensible. The AutoFormat command allows you to apply a set of formatting characteristics to the contents of cells or to a cell or range itself. Sometimes, however, you may want to exert more precise control over the appearance of a cell or range than AutoFormat permits. Excel gives you the ability to fill cells and ranges with colors and patterns, and outline them with special borders.

Do It!

Kay wants to experiment with adding a color pattern and a border to the title of her worksheet. She will then undo her experiment.

1 Click cell **A2** to select the merged cell that contains the worksheet's title.

2 Click the arrow on the right edge of the **Fill Color** button. A color palette will open below the button.

3 Click the **Rose** color square in the bottom-left corner of the palette. The palette will close and the merged title cell will be filled with Rose.

4 Click **Format**, then click **Cells**. The **Format Cells** dialog box will open.

5 Click the **Border** tab to bring it to the front of the dialog box. In the **Presets** section of the tab, click the **Outline** button. In the **Line Style** section, select the dashed line (fourth down in the second column).

6 Click the **Color** selection arrow and choose the **Dark Red** square from the palette that appears. The Border tab should now look like **Figure 3-19**.

7 Click the **Patterns** tab to bring it to the front. Notice that the Rose color square is selected and shown in the **Sample** box because it has already been applied to the active cell.

8 Click the **Pattern** selection arrow. A color palette that includes patterns at the top will open. Click the **Diagonal Stripe** pattern (fourth from the left in the second row). The Pattern tab should now look like **Figure 3-20**.

9 Click [OK] to apply the border and pattern to the selected cell, and then deselect the cell, which should resemble **Figure 3-21**.

10 Click the arrow on the right edge of the Undo button and highlight the three Format Cells operations you just performed. Click the mouse to undo the actions.

More

The Font Color, Fill Color, and Borders buttons are all "loaded" with the last option (color or border type) you applied, which is displayed as part of the button's icon. To apply this option again, you do not need to click the button's arrow to open its palette. Simply click on the button itself.

Figure 3-19 Border tab

Selected line style for border

Selected color for border

Figure 3-20 Patterns tab

Sample box shows color and pattern

Figure 3-21 Cell formatted with color, pattern, and border

Excel 2000

Practice

Open a new workbook. Then fill the range A1:D5 with the color Aqua, add an inside, dotted border to the range, and fill cell B2 with a yellow vertical stripe pattern. Do not save this exercise.

Hot Tip

Color and patterns should be used carefully as overuse and misuse can damage the effectiveness of your spreadsheet, as you may have discovered while completing this Skill.

Shortcuts

Function	Button/Mouse	Menu	Keyboard
Merge cells and center contents	▦		
Merge cells		Click Format, then click Cells, then click Alignment	[Ctrl]+[1]
Make a label bold	B	Click Format, then click Cells, then click Font	[Ctrl]+[B]
Italicize a label	I	Click Format, then click Cells, then click Font	[Ctrl]+[I]
Underline a label	U	Click Format, then click Cells, then click Font	[Ctrl]+[U]
Add color to a label	▲·	Click Format, then click Cells, then click Font	[Ctrl]+[1]
Comma Style	,	Click Format, then click Style	
Currency Style	$	Click Format, then click Style	
Percent Style	%	Click Format, then click Style	
Increase or Decrease decimal places	⊞ or ⊞		

Identify Key Features

Name the items indicated by callouts in **Figure 3-22.**

Figure 3-22 Formatting features

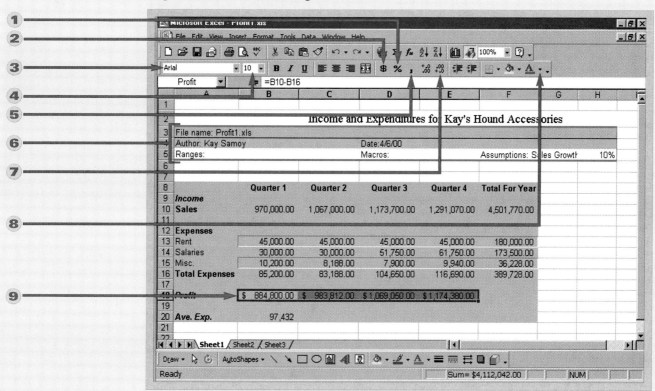

Select The Best Answer

10. Allows you to select a named range quickly and accurately

11. Contains a tab with options for changing font, font style, and font size

12. Combines the contents of multiple cells into one cell

13. Lets you add a set of predetermined formatting options to a spreadsheet

14. Contains the Bold, Italic, and Underline buttons

15. A group of two or more cells

16. Indicates that a particular formatting style is applied to the current selection

17. A blank column at the end of a defined range

a. Indented button

b. Formatting toolbar

c. Dummy column

d. Format Cells dialog box

e. AutoFormat command

f. Name box

g. Range

h. Merge and Center button

Complete the Statement

18. All of the following are effects available on the Font tab of the Format Cells dialog box except:

   a. Strikethrough

   b. Strikescript

   c. Superscript

   d. Subscript

19. An appropriate way to express a range address is:

   a. B9/E9

   b. B9;E9

   c. B9-E9

   d. B9:E9

20. A range name may not contain:

   a. Uppercase letters

   b. Labels used in the spreadsheet

   c. Spaces

   d. Numbers

21. The Formatting toolbar offers all of the following formatting styles except:

   a. Currency Style

   b. Percentage Style

   c. Fraction Style

   d. Comma Style

22. The standard width of a worksheet column is:

   a. 8.43 characters

   b. 13.00 characters

   c. 13.5 characters

   d. 255 characters

23. All of the following can be done from the Insert menu except:

   a. Insert a blank row

   b. Insert a blank column

   c. Define and name a range

   d. Apply an AutoFormat

24. A 72 point character would be equal to:

   a. 1 inch

   b. 1 foot

   c. 8.43 centimeters

   d. 8.43 inches

25. 3D Effects 2 is a type of:

   a. Cell value

   b. Range name

   c. AutoFormat

   d. Function

26. All of the following are examples of series data you can enter in a worksheet except:

   a. Linear

   b. Growth

   c. Currency

   d. AutoFill

27. The largest font size in points is:

   a. 409

   b. 256

   c. 72

   d. 8.43

Interactivity

Test Your Skills

1. Define and name the ranges in a spreadsheet:

   a. Open the file Test 2.xls that you created at the end of the previous lesson.

   b. Define and name the following ranges using the name box: Class, Activities, Meals, Studying/Homework, Leisure, and Sleep.

   c. Define and name the following ranges by opening the Define name dialog box from the Insert menu: Monday, Tuesday, Wednesday, Thursday, Friday, Saturday, Sunday, Total Hours, and Average.

2. Format cell labels in a spreadsheet:

   a. Change the font of the title of your worksheet to Times New Roman, and then change its size to 12 point.

   b. Merge and center the title across the first ten columns of the worksheet.

   c. Add bold formatting to the days of the week labels. Italicize and underline the Total Hours and Average labels.

   d. Change the font color of the daily activities labels in Column A to red, and then make them bold.

3. Adjust the columns and rows in your spreadsheet:

   a. Click and drag the right border of Column A until the column is 18.00 characters wide.

   b. Click and drag the right border of the Wednesday column until the entire label "Wednesday" is visible.

   c. Double-click with the mouse to automatically resize the Total Hours column so that its label fits.

   d. Add an extra row between the documentation and data sections of your worksheet.

4. Add advanced formatting to your spreadsheet:

   a. Reduce all values in the Average column to three decimal places.

   b. Apply Comma Style to all values in the Total Hours column.

   c. Apply the AutoFormat 3D Effects 1 to the documentation section of the worksheet.

   d. Apply the AutoFormat Classic 3 to the data section of your worksheet, but preserve the font and width/height that the worksheet already has.

   e. Add an outside, solid blue border to the merged title cell.

   f. Fill the title cell with the color orange and the pattern Thin Horizontal Stripe.

   g. Save the file as Test 3.xls.

Interactivity (continued)

Problem Solving

1. Utilize the knowledge and skills you have acquired about spreadsheet design to keep yourself on track as you work toward earning a diploma. Using Excel, create a worksheet that displays your graduation requirements and the means by which you are fulfilling them. Include courses you may have already taken, your current courses, and the courses you will need and want to take in the future. Also include data such as the total number of credits you need to graduate and the percentage you have so far. Calculate how many credits you will need to average each academic semester. Then see if your actual numbers are on pace. Finally, be sure to take advantage of Excel's formatting features to enhance the organization and appearance of your spreadsheet. Save the file as Solved 3-Grad.xls.

2. Open Solved-HR2.xls, a file you saved at the end of the previous lesson. Define and name all relevant ranges in the worksheet. Format the entire worksheet in a professional manner, using both independent formatting techniques and one instance of the AutoFormat command. Make sure to employ Currency Style where appropriate, and do not allow this formatting to be overwritten by an AutoFormat. Print the worksheet and save the file as Solved-HR3.xls.

3. Open Solved-Rest2.xls, the other file you saved at the end of the previous lesson. Delete the column that holds the data for the average hours worked per day by each member of the waitstaff. Delete all of the labels that refer to days of the week in the schedule and replace them using an AutoFill. Apply bold formatting to all column heading labels and make their text green. Italicize all row heading labels and change their font to 11 point, Arial Narrow text. Define all horizontal ranges using the Name Box, and vertical ranges using menu commands. Save the file as Solved-Rest3.xls and print a hard copy.

4 . Replicate the worksheet shown below to the best of your ability.

Then, delete Column B, insert a row between the numbers section and the days section, insert three rows between the days section and the red pattern section, and finally, delete the extra cells that were added to Column A. Print the resulting worksheet.

L E S S O N

4

INSERTING OBJECTS AND CHARTS

Though the labels and values you enter into a spreadsheet serve as its core, other objects may represent certain data better or simply illustrate it further. Inserting these objects can break up the monotony of row after row of numbers and allow you to explain or highlight aspects of your spreadsheet that might otherwise go unnoticed.

You can insert a number of objects into your worksheet for the purpose of annotating specific information. These include text boxes, shapes such as arrows and connectors, and comments. Text boxes can be any size, but will obscure the portions of the worksheet behind them. Comments are similar to text boxes, but can be hidden from view. All graphics can be formatted and manipulated in a variety of ways.

One very effective way of enhancing your worksheet visually is to add a chart. The Chart Wizard can guide you through the process of creating a graphical representation of a data series that you select from your Excel worksheet. Charts can be moved, resized, and formatted. You can even change a chart's type and characteristics after it has been created. In addition, individual chart elements can be customized for emphasis and clarity.

CASE STUDY
In this lesson, Kay will strengthen her spreadsheet by inserting graphics and creating a chart using the Chart Wizard. Afterward, she will use some of Excel's advanced printing features to print a new copy of her worksheet.

Inserting Text Boxes

Concept

Text can also be inserted into a worksheet within a **text box**. Creating text boxes allows you to add passages of any size and appearance without the constraints of a cell in the worksheet. A text box is an independent object. Therefore, you can use it to reference data without affecting the data.

Do It!

Kay wants to insert a text box into her worksheet to emphasize the growth in projected Quarter 4 sales.

1 Click View, highlight Toolbars, then click Drawing if it is not already checked. The Drawing toolbar will be visible.

2 Click the Text Box button ▣ on the Drawing toolbar. The pointer will change to the text cursor ↓ when it is in the workspace, allowing you to create a text box.

3 Click in cell E6, just below the green line where you want the top right corner of the text box to appear, then drag down and to the right to cell F7, until the box you have created is approximately one cell long by two cells high, like the one shown in **Figure 4-1**. When you release the mouse button, the borders of the box will become dotted and eight small squares called sizing handles will appear. There will be a sizing handle at each corner and one in the center of each side of the text box. A blinking insertion point will also appear in the text box.

4 Type Up 33% from Quarter 1 to enter it into the text box.

5 Click elsewhere in the worksheet to deselect the text box. Your worksheet should now resemble the one shown in **Figure 4-2**.

6 Save your worksheet.

More

The primary advantage of using text boxes is their flexibility. Text boxes may be easily moved, resized, or reformatted, without affecting the appearance or content of any other part of the worksheet. When text is being entered, a text box acts as a small word processing window. If there is not enough room on a line to fit a word, the text will **wrap** and continue on the next line. If the text box you have made is not large enough to accommodate the text as you are entering it, then the text will scroll upward, without changing the size or location of the box, to allow the additional text to be entered. The text box will have to be enlarged manually to view all of the text it contains. This can be accomplished through the use of the sizing handles, by clicking and dragging the handle in the desired direction of movement, expanding or reducing the size of the box.

Once a text box has been created, it is not fixed in place, but may be moved anywhere on the worksheet. To move a text box to another part of the worksheet, click the frame of a selected text box (not on a sizing handle) to select its frame, and then drag the text box to the desired destination.

Figure 4-1 Creating a text box

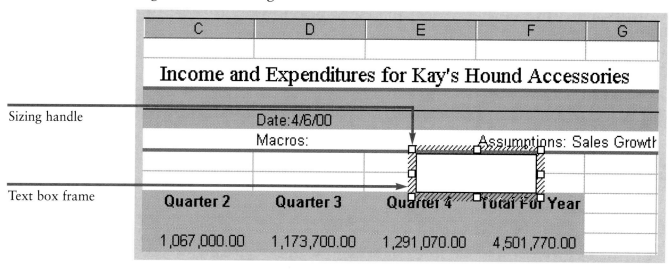

Sizing handle

Text box frame

Figure 4-2 Text box with text

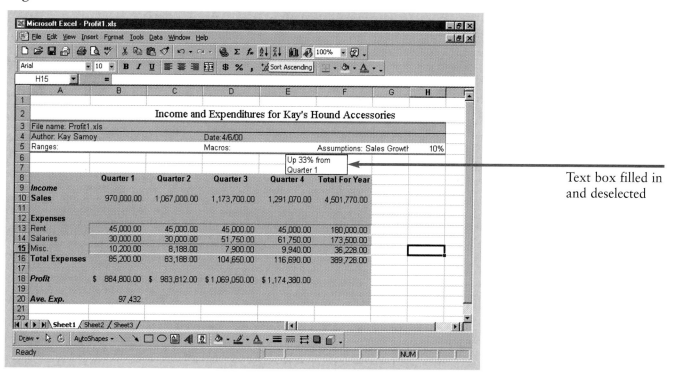

Text box filled in
and deselected

Practice

To practice inserting text boxes, open the
practice file **Practice–Lesson 4.xls**, save
the file as **MyPractice 4.xls**, then follow
the instructions on the **Prac4-1** tab.

Hot Tip

Text boxes are always visible, and hide the
portion of the worksheet behind them. Text
boxes can overlap each other, however,
and their order can be changed by right-
clicking one and choosing an option from
the Order submenu that appears.

Enhancing Graphics

Concept

Graphic objects that you have inserted, such as lines, text boxes, or pictures, can be modified to alter and improve their appearance.

Do It!

Kay will add a callout arrow and color to the text box that she inserted in the previous Skill.

1 Click the Arrow button ▧ on the Drawing toolbar. It will indent, and the mouse pointer will appear as a thin cross + when it is over the worksheet.

2 Position the pointer just after the **1** in the text box, then click and drag to cell **E10**, the Sales value for Quarter 4. When the mouse button is released, the line that was being drawn becomes fixed, and an arrowhead appears at the end.

3 Click the text box to select it. Its frame becomes a thick hatched line.

4 Click the text box's frame (but not a sizing handle) to select the frame. It changes from a hatched to a dotted border.

5 Click the arrow on the Fill Color button ▧▾ on the drawing toolbar to open the Fill Color palette.

6 Click the pale blue square in the bottom row of the palette to select it. The text box's background will change to match the selected color.

7 Click the arrow you drew to select it. A sizing handle appears at each end of the arrow to indicate its selection.

8 Click the Line Color drop-down arrow ▧▾ to open the Line Color palette, and select the red square in the middle of the first column. The arrow will change to match the color of the selected square.

9 Click elsewhere in the worksheet to deselect the arrow. The text box and arrow should now resemble the ones shown in **Figure 4-3**.

More

The Format menu is context-sensitive, which means that its content changes based on the item that is selected. When a cell is active, the Format menu contains commands for altering a cell, while a selected AutoShape will cause another set of commands to appear on the Format menu. Objects that are inserted into an Excel document, such as lines, AutoShapes, and Clip Art, all have their own formatting dialog boxes with tabs relating to the selected object.

The Format Text Box command, available on the Format menu when a text box is selected, opens the Format Text Box dialog box shown in **Figure 4-4**. This dialog box contains seven tabs with options for altering many aspects of a text box. While many of the controls found in the Format Text Box dialog box have toolbar buttons, the dialog box allows more precise and comprehensive control over such aspects the size of the text box, the internal margins of the text box, and the orientation of text within a text box.

Figure 4-3 Enhancing worksheet graphics

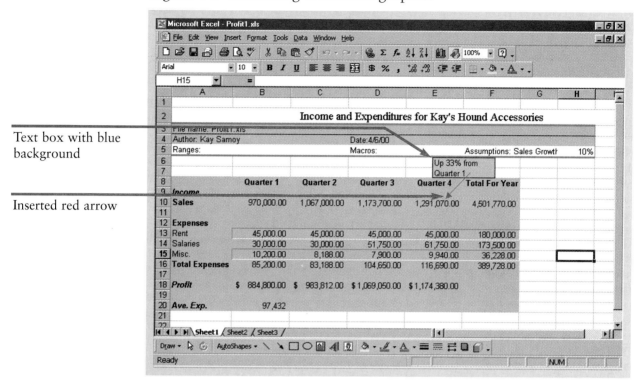

Text box with blue background

Inserted red arrow

Excel 2000

Figure 4-4 Format Text Box dialog box

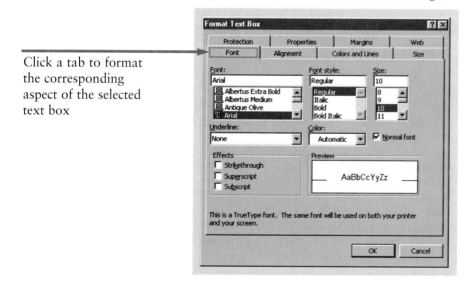

Click a tab to format the corresponding aspect of the selected text box

Practice

To practice enhancing graphics follow the instructions on the **Prac4-2** tab of the practice file **MyPractice 4.xls**.

Hot Tip

You can open an object's formatting dialog box by double-clicking it. Double-clicking a text box's frame will open the dialog box shown above, but double-clicking in the text box will only allow you to alter the text itself.

Adding Comments

Concept

A comment is an electronic note that can be attached to a cell. Comments are hidden from view until the mouse pointer is over a cell that contains one. Comments are useful for documenting information or making notes. If multiple people will be using a spreadsheet, comments can be used as a way to share information.

Do It!

Since there is not enough room in the documentation section of her worksheet to list all of the named ranges, Kay will insert a comment containing the range names.

1 Click cell **A5** to make it active.

2 Click **Insert**, then click **Comment**. An active text box with the name of the designated user and an insertion point, shown in **Figure 4-5**, will appear next to the selected cell. The text box will have an arrow pointing to the cell it references and a red triangle will appear in the upper-right corner of the cell indicating that it contains a comment.

3 Select the contents of the cell by dragging the I-beam over the text in the box.

4 Type **Kay Samoy:** and then press [Enter]. This is to indicate that Kay is the author of the comment. Notice that the name that first appeared in the comment box appears in the status bar. This can be changed from the General tab of the Options dialog box available on the Tools menu.

5 Type the following range names, pressing [Enter] after each: **Miscellaneous, Profit, Quarter 1, Quarter 2, Quarter 3, Quarter 4, Rent, Salaries, Sales, Total Expenses.** The text will scroll as you type hiding the first few entries.

6 Drag the midpoint sizing handle of the bottom edge of the comment box down until it is approximately even with row 13. When you release the mouse button the comment box will expand so that all the text will be visible as shown in **Figure 4-6**.

7 Click elsewhere in the worksheet to deselect cell A5 and hide the comment.

8 Position the pointer over cell **A5**. The comment will be displayed.

9 Save your workbook.

More

Like cells and text boxes, comment boxes and the text they contain can be formatted. Right-clicking a cell that contains a comment opens a pop-up menu with a command for editing and deleting comments. These commands activate the comment connected to the selected cell. Double-clicking the comment's border will open the Format Comment dialog box, and clicking in the comment box will allow you to manipulated the text itself. The Reviewing toolbar, whose buttons are listed in **Table 4-1**, contains commands for displaying and navigating among comments. It can be activated from the Toolbars submenu on the View menu. Once a comment has been opened for editing, you can move it anywhere in the worksheet by clicking and dragging its border; a line will always run from the comment to its parent cell.

Figure 4-5 Adding a comment to a cell

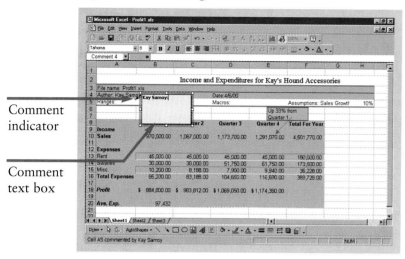

Comment indicator

Comment text box

Figure 4-6 Kay's comment

Kay Samoy:
Miscellaneous
Profit
Quarter 1
Quarter 2
Quarter 3
Quarter 4
Rent
Salaries
Sales
Total Expenses

Table 4-1 Reviewing toolbar buttons

BUTTON	NAME	FUNCTION
	New Comment	Opens a new comment
	Edit Comment	Displays the comment with an insertion point in the comment pane
	Previous Comment	Displays the previous comment
	Next Comment	Displays the next comment
	Show/Hide Comment	Leaves a comment visible even when the mouse pointer is not over the selected parent cell; deselecting this button returns the comment to its default hidden state
	Show/Hide All Comments	Shows or hides all comments on the worksheet
	Delete Comment	Permanently removes a comment and its reference mark in the parent cell

Practice

To practice adding comments, follow the instructions on the **Prac4-3** tab of the practice file **MyPractice 4.xls**.

Hot Tip

Either the New Comment button or the Edit Comment button will appear on the Reviewing toolbar, depending on whether or not the selected cell already contains a comment.

Creating a Chart

Concept

Charts are graphics that represent values and their relationships. Using charts you can quickly identify trends in data, and see the contrasts among values. Excel allows you to portray data easily using a variety of two- and three-dimensional chart styles. These styles give data immediate meaning, unlike data in its raw form, which generally requires studying.

Do It!

Kay wants to show the values for Rent, Salaries, and Miscellaneous expenses as percentages of her total yearly expenses.

1. Select the range F13:F15. These are the values that are required to create the chart.

2. Click the **Chart Wizard** button 📊 on the Standard toolbar. The Chart Wizard dialog box opens, as shown in **Figure 4-7**, with the Column chart type selected. If the Office Assistant appears, close it by clicking the **No, I do not want help now** option as the Assistant is not necessary for this Skill.

3. Click **Pie** in the Chart type list box. The Chart sub-types will change to show different type of pie charts.

4. Click Next > . The Wizard will advance to its second step with a pie chart representing the selected data displayed. If you had not already selected cells you could enter which cells to include in your chart in the data range text box.

5. Click the **Series** tab to bring it the front of the stack.

6. Click the **Category Labels** text box to activate it. A flashing insertion point will appear in the text box so you can name the categories for you chart.

7. Click the **Collapse Dialog** button 📊. The dialog box will shrink so only the Category Labels text box is shown. Collapsing the dialog box allows you to view more of the worksheet so you can easily select the cells to be inserted as the labels for your chart's categories.

8. Select A13:A15. An animated border will surround the selected range, a ScreenTip will display the size of the selection, and the range will appear in the collapsed dialog box, as shown in **Figure 4-8**.

Figure 4-7 Chart Wizard dialog box: Step 1

Click here to select a chart type

Name and description of the selected chart sub-type

Click here to select a chart sub-type

Click here to to preview the chart sub-type using data extracted from your worksheet

Figure 4-8   Selecting the category labels

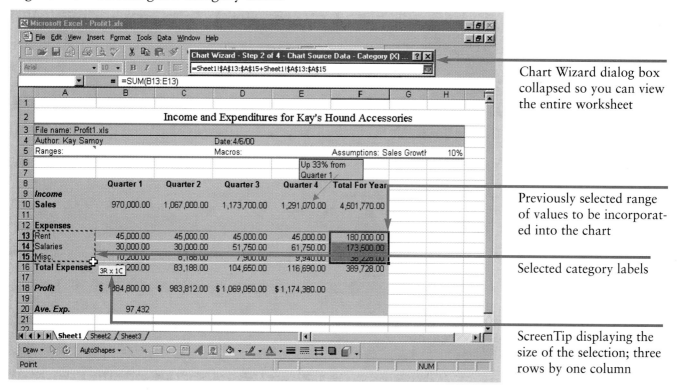

Chart Wizard dialog box collapsed so you can view the entire worksheet

Previously selected range of values to be incorporated into the chart

Selected category labels

ScreenTip displaying the size of the selection; three rows by one column

Creating
a Chart (continued)

Do It!

9 Click the Expand Dialog button 🔳 to bring the full dialog box into view.

10 Click ⌈Next >⌉. The third step of the Wizard will be shown.

11 Click the Chart tile text box, then type Breakdown of Expenses. The title you have entered will appear in the preview area to the right of the text box. The other other text boxes are grayed out since they are not applicable to the chosen chart type.

12 Click the Legend tab to bring it to the front of the stack.

13 Click the Show legend check box to deselect this option, as you will be labeling the chart later.

14 Click the Data Labels tab to bring it to the front of the stack.

15 Click the Show label and percent radio button. Labels and percentages will appear in the preview.

16 Click ⌈Next >⌉ to advance to the last step of the Wizard. As you can see in Figure 4-9, the As object in radio button is selected, indicating that the chart will appear in the current worksheet as opposed to a new one.

17 Click ⌈Finish⌉. The Chart Wizard dialog box will close, your chart will be displayed in the center of your worksheet, and the Chart toolbar will appear in the Excel window, as shown in Figure 4-10.

18 Save your workbook.

More

When the chart is selected, the Data menu is replaced by the Chart menu. The first four commands on the Chart menu open dialog boxes that are similar to the steps of the Chart Wizard. This allows you to alter any of the characteristics of the chart without having to recreate it with the Chart Wizard. The Add Data command lets you append the ranges that are displayed.

Figure 4-9 Chart Wizard dialog box: Step 4

Click to create
chart in its own,
new worksheet

Figure 4-10 Finished chart

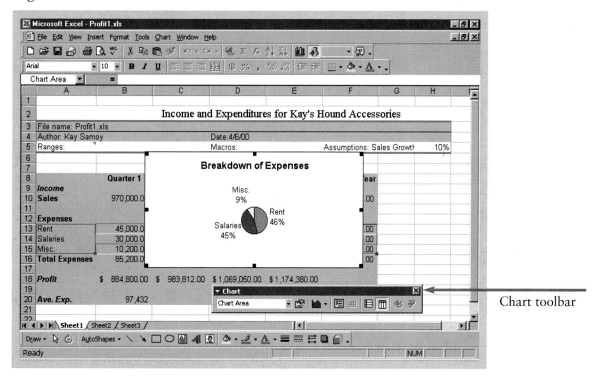

Chart toolbar

Practice

To practice creating a chart, follow the
instructions on the **Prac4-4** tab of the practice file **MyPractice 4.xls**.

Hot Tip

When a chart is selected, ranges that it references will be selected in the worksheet.
You can add or subtract cells from the
ranges portrayed in the chart by dragging a
selected range's fill handle. Moving the cell
pointer selects a new range.

Moving and Resizing a Chart

Concept

Once you have created a chart, you can change its size and location in the worksheet so that it complements your data without obstructing it. While a chart may be the focus of your worksheet, it is still just one part of the overall presentation.

Do It!

Kay wants to move the chart below the main data of her worksheet and then resize it so that its boundaries match those of existing columns and rows.

1. Click the selected chart and drag it down and to the left until the upper-left corner of the dotted border is in cell A21 (see **Figure 4-11**). As you move the mouse the pointer will change to the movement pointer ⁺↕⁺ and the dotted border will indicate where the chart will appear when the mouse button is released. The worksheet will scroll upward when the mouse pointer is dragged below the document window.

2. Scroll downward until the entire chart can be seen in the document window, if it is not already.

3. Position the mouse pointer over the midpoint sizing handle of the right edge of the chart, then click and drag the edge of the chart to the left until it is even with the boundary between columns C and D. The chart will adjust itself so it remains centered and proportional in its box.

4. Using the midpoint sizing handle on the bottom of the chart, drag the chart edge to the boundary between rows 34 and 35. Notice that the chart elements expand slightly to fill the larger area. Your chart should resemble the one shown in **Figure 4-11**.

5. Save your workbook.

More

Table 4-2 below summarizes different techniques you can use to move and resize charts and other objects.

Table 4-2 Object resizing techniques

ACTION	TO
Press [Shift] while dragging the chart	Constrain a chart's movement to only the horizontal or vertical
Press [Ctrl] while dragging the chart	Copy the chart to another place in the worksheet
Press [Shift] while dragging a corner sizing handle	Constrain a chart's aspect ratio when resizing it
Press [Ctrl] while dragging a sizing handle	Maintain a chart's center point when resizing
Press [Ctrl]+[Shift] while dragging a corner sizing handle	Maintain a chart's center point and aspect ratio when resizing

Figure 4-11 Repositioned and resized chart

Chart elements adjust
to fit the redefined
chart area

Practice

To practice moving and resizing a chart,
follow the instructions on the **Prac4-5** tab
of the practice file **MyPractice 4.xls**.

Hot Tip

As you move the mouse pointer over various elements of the chart, ScreenTips will
appear with a brief explanation of that
item. These ScreenTips may be disabled by
pressing [Alt].

Formatting a Chart

Concept

After a chart has been created, many of its features may be altered. The color and location of chart elements can be changed, and formatting can be applied to text.

Do It!

Kay wants to emphasize that her company has met its goal of keeping miscellaneous expenses under of 10% of total expenses by isolating the corresponding pie slice in the chart and changing its color. She would also like to format the chart title.

1   Click the pie in your chart to make it active. Three sizing handles will appear indicating its selection.

2   Click the Miscellaneous pie slice to select it.

3   Click and drag the Miscellaneous slice away from the pie so the point of the triangle is even with the former border of the pie. Notice that the slice's label moves to accommodate the slice's new position. (See **Figure 4-13**.)

4   Double-click the Miscellaneous pie slice. The Format Data Point dialog box opens.

5   Click the Patterns tab, shown in **Figure 4-12**, to bring it to front if it is not already there.

6   In the Area section of the tab, click the yellow box in the bottom row, beneath the currently selected color. The sample color, shown in the lower left of the tab, will change to illustrate the newly selected color.

7   Click ⬚ OK ⬚. The dialog box closes, and the chart will appear with the new color applied to the Miscellaneous slice, as seen in **Figure 4-13**.

8   Double-click the chart's title, Breakdown of Expenses, to open the Format Chart Title dialog box.

9   On the Patterns tab, click the Shadow check box to activate it.

10 Click ⬚ OK ⬚. The dialog box closes, and the chart's title now appears in a box with a shadow applied to it. Click elsewhere in the worksheet to deselect the chart title; your chart should now resemble the one shown in **Figure 4-13**.

More

Double-clicking any element of a chart will open a dialog box that enables you to format and alter the selected chart element. Depending upon what item is selected, the available tabs of this dialog box will provide the appropriate formatting options. Elements may also be selected and their formatting dialog boxes opened using the Chart toolbar, pictured in **Figure 4-14**.

On the Patterns tab of chart element formatting dialog boxes there is a Fill Effects button that lets you apply advanced formatting options such as gradients, textures, patterns, or pictures to the selected element.

Figure 4-12 Format Data Point dialog box

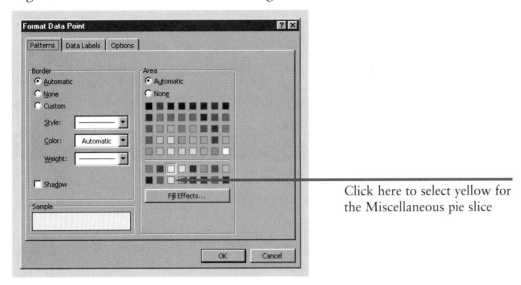

Click here to select yellow for
the Miscellaneous pie slice

Excel 2000

Figure 4-13 Formatted chart elements

Chart title formatted with a shadow

Miscellaneous slice with new
color and dragged away from
the pie

Figure 4-14 Chart toolbar

To practice formatting a chart, follow the
instructions on the **Prac4-6** tab of the practice file **MyPractice 4.xls**.

Hot Tip

Chart titles and labels may be dragged to
new locations in the chart area, as can the
chart itself.

Changing a Chart's Type

Concept

Excel allows you to change a chart's type while maintaining the same referenced data series. For example, a bar chart can be easily converted to a line graph to more effectively present the data it contains. You may also switch between variants of the same chart type, called sub-types, that will make your chart easier to read.

Do It!

Kay would like to display her pie chart with a 3-D visual effect.

1. With the chart selected, click Chart, then click Chart Type. The Chart Type dialog box opens with the Standard Types tab in front, with the selected chart's type and sub-type selected (if the Standard Types tab is not in front, click it now).

2. Click the second chart sub-type, Pie with a 3-D visual effect. It will become highlighted, and a description of it will appear in the area beneath the Chart sub-types.

3. Click [OK]. The dialog box closes, and your chart appears with the new sub-type applied, as shown in **Figure 4-15**.

4. Click Chart, then click 3-D View. The 3-D View dialog box, shown in **Figure 4-16**, appears with the current elevation of 15 degrees selected.

5. Click [⬆] twice to increase the chart's elevation to 25 degrees. The chart in the preview box will pivot, illustrating the effect that the changes you are making will have on the chart.

6. Click [OK]. The dialog box closes and the chart reflects the changes that you have made, as shown in **Figure 4-17**. Save your changes.

More

Table 4-3 Chart types

CHART TYPE	DESCRIPTION	EXAMPLE
📊 Column	Data changes over time or quantitative comparisons among items	Quarterly income projections
📊 Bar	Similar to a column chart, but horizontal orientation places more value on the X value	Individual sales performance
📈 Line	Trends in data at fixed intervals	Tracking stock trends
🥧 Pie	The percentage each value contributes to the whole. Used for a single data series	Budgets, chief exports of a country
📉 XY (Scatter)	Comparative relationships between seemingly dissimilar data	Scientific data analysis
📊 Surface	The range of intersections between two sets of data	Optimal fuel consumption

Figure 4-15 Pie with a 3-D visual effect

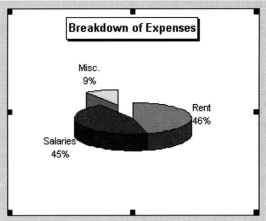

Excel 2000

Figure 4-16 Chart toolbar

Click here to increase
or decrease chart
elevation below

Preview changes here

Click to revert to chart's
original elevation and
rotation

Click buttons to rotate chart

Figure 4-17 Chart with increased elevation

Practice

To practice changing a chart's type, follow
the instructions on the **Prac4-7** tab of
MyPractice 4.xls.

Hot Tip

The Chart Type drop-down arrow on
the Chart toolbar allows you to quickly
change the selected chart from one type to
another.

Using Advanced Printing Features

Concept

A worksheet, especially one that contains embedded objects such as a chart, may not always fit on a standard printed page using the default printing settings. Excel allows you to preview and change page orientation so as to accommodate different arrangements of data. You can also choose to print specific parts of a spreadsheet such as a chart, a page, the active worksheet, or the entire workbook. As in many programs, you can access these options through the Page Setup dialog box and the Print dialog box. Using these dialog boxes in conjuntion with the Print Preview will allow you to get the most out of printing your work.

Do It!

Kay wants to change the page orientation so her entire worksheet will fit onto one printed page.

1. Click outside of the chart to deselect it.

2. Click the Print Preview button . Your worksheet will be displayed in Print Preview mode. Notice that the status bar reads Preview: Page 1 of 2, and the Next button is active indicating that there is another page.

3. Click in the upper-right corner of the document preview with the magnification pointer. As you can see from **Figure 4-18**, the worksheet will appear magnified in the window with the worksheet title and cell labels cropped, making it apparent that the entire worksheet does not fit on the page.

4. Click Setup.... The Page Setup dialog box will appear as shown in **Figure 4-19**.

5. Click the Landscape radio button in the Orientation section of the dialog box.

6. Click OK. The dialog box will close and you will see that the entire worksheet is now visible on the preview page.

Figure 4-18 Magnified worksheet in Print Preview

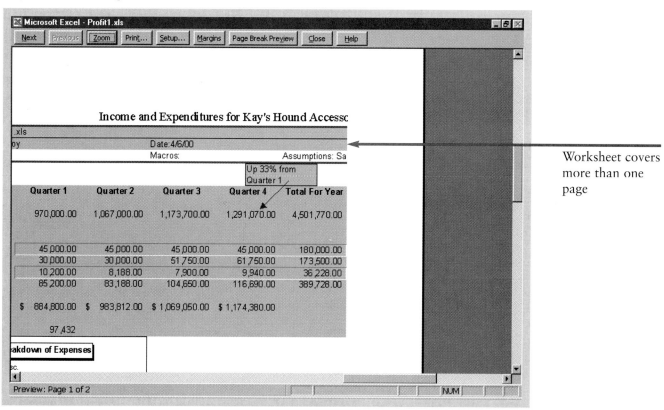

Worksheet covers more than one page

Excel 2000

Figure 4-19 Page Setup dialog box

Allows you to print worksheet as a percentage of its actual size

Click Landscape to print worksheet with horizontal page orientation

Using Advanced Printing Features

(continued)

Do It!

7 Click the preview to zoom out. The entire page will appear horizontally in the window but the status bar will still read Page 1 of 2, as shown in **Figure 4-20** (if this is not the case, exit Print Preview, change the widths of columns A through H to at least 14 characters, and then return to Print Preview and continue).

8 Click **Next**. A blank page appears. This is page contains blank cells that belong to cell A2 which was merged to encompass the range A2:J2 when the title was centered. It is not necessary to print this second page as it only contains blank cells.

9 Click **Print...**. Print Preview will close, you will be returned to normal view, and the Print dialog box will open.

10 In the Print range section of the dialog box, click the up arrow of the **From** text box ▢ ▲▼ . A 1 will appear selected in the box designating it as the first page to print, and the Page(s) radio button will be selected.

11 Click the up arrow in the To text box. A 1 will appear selected in the box telling Excel to stop printing after page 1.

12 Click **OK**. The Print dialog box will close and the document will be sent to the printer.

13 Save your workbook.

More

Excel's print function allows you select the area or item you wish to print. Therefore, you do not have to send an entire worksheet to the printer if you wish to have a hard copy of a smaller portion. With a chart selected, the Print dialog box will have the Selected Chart radio button active in the Print what area so that only the chart, and not the remaining data of the worksheet, will be printed. Likewise, the Print Preview will display just the chart, as this view shows you exactly how the information will be printed with the current settings. If you select a chart, then click the Page Setup command found on the File menu, the Page Setup dialog box will open with a tab labeled Chart. Compare this dialog box shown in **Figure 4-21** to the one shown in **Figure 4-19**. This tab contains options concerning the chart's printed size and print quality.

Figure 4-20 Preview of worksheet in landscape orientation

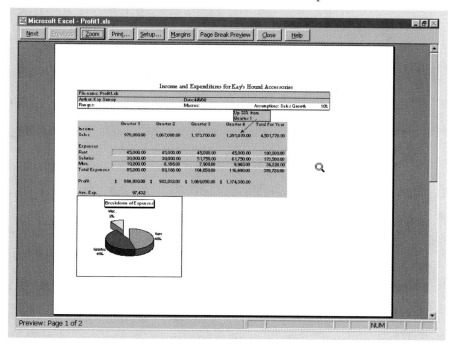

Figure 4-21 Page Setup dialog box when a chart is selected

Practice

To practice using advanced printing features, follow the instructions on the **Prac4-8** tab of the practice file **MyPractice 4.xls**.

Hot Tip

The Page Break Preview command, found on the View menu, allows you to adjust what portion of the worksheet will fit on one printed page. The data contained in the worksheet will be reduced to fit on the page if you expand the print range.

Shortcuts

Function	Button/Mouse	Menu	Keyboard
Drawing toolbar		Click View, then highlight Toolbars, then click Drawing	
Chart Wizard		Click Insert, then click Chart	
Format chart area (or selected chart object)		Click Format, then click Selected Chart Area (or other object)	[Ctrl]+[1]
Change chart type		Click Chart, then click Chart Type	
Add/Remove chart legend		Click Chart, then click Chart Options	
Plot chart data series by row		Click Chart, then click Source Data	
Plot chart data series by column		Click Chart, then click Source Data	

Identify Key Features

Name the items indicated by callouts in **Figure 4-22**.

Figure 4-22 Identify features of the Excel screen

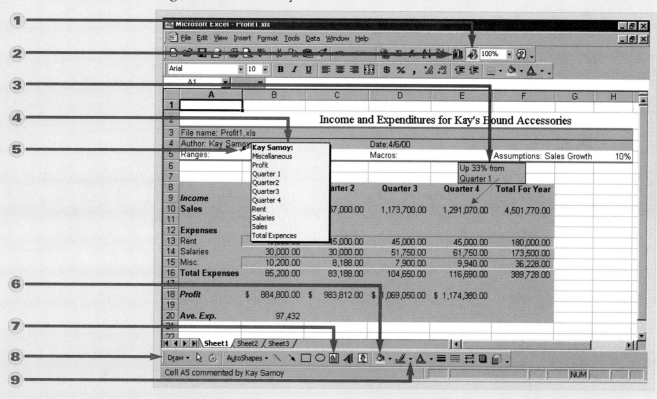

Excel 2000

Select The Best Answer

10. Allows you to add text to a worksheet without worrying about cell constraints

11. Reduces the size of a dialog box so that you can easily view the worksheet

12. Appears along with your chart when you complete the Chart Wizard

13. Allows you to format any chart element from a dialog box

14. Indicates that a chart will be printed as opposed to the entire worksheet

15. An electronic note attached to a cell

16. A graphic that represents values and their relationships

17. Horizontal page orientation

18. Allows you to add colors and gradients to chart elements

a. Collapse dialog button

b. Double-clicking

c. Patterns tab

d. Chart toolbar

e. Selected Chart radio button

f. Landscape

g. Text box

h. Comment

i. Chart

Quiz (continued)

Complete the Statement

19. To change the user name that appears on comments, go to the:

    a. Summary tab in the Properties dialog box

    b. Replace dialog box

    c. Define Name dialog box

    d. General tab in the Options dialog box

20. The Arrow tool can be found on the:

    a. Standard toolbar

    b. Formatting toolbar

    c. Drawing toolbar

    d. Shapes toolbar

21. To navigate among comments, use the:

    a. Comment toolbar

    b. Reviewing toolbar

    c. Standard toolbar

    d. Vertical scroll bar

22. All of the following are standard chart types except:

    a. Pie

    b. Doughnut

    c. Line

    d. Volume

23. You can add a title to a chart by using the:

    a. Chart Options dialog box

    b. Source Data dialog box

    c. Format Chart area dialog box

    d. Chart Type dialog box

24. You may change all of the following chart aspects from the 3-D View dialog box with the exception of:

    a. Elevation

    b. Rotation

    c. Height

    d. Location

25. To maintain a chart's center point when resizing it:

    a. Press [Ctrl] while dragging the chart

    b. Press [Shift] while dragging a sizing handle

    c. Press [Ctrl] while dragging a sizing handle

    d. Press [Tab] while dragging a sizing handle

26. If the text in a text box exceeds the size of the box:

    a. The text box will resize itself

    b. The beginning of the text will be deleted

    c. The text will scroll up

    d. No more text can be added.

27. The small squares in the corners and middle of each side of a comment or chart are called:

    a. Sizing handles

    b. Fill handles

    c. Jug handles

    d. Frames

Interactivity

Test Your Skills

1. Add objects and graphics to a spreadsheet:

   a. Open the file **Test 3.xls** that you created at the end of the previous Lesson.

   b. Add a text box that says **Best day for relaxation and errands** above the day of the week column of your choice.

   c. Use the **Fill Color** palette to add color to the text box.

   d. Draw an **arrow** from the text box to the appropriate day of the week label.

   e. Use the **Line Color** palette to add color to the arrow.

   f. Enter a **comment** that displays the names of all your defined ranges in the cell that contains the Ranges label.

2. Create a chart based on your worksheet data:

   a. Select the **Average** range in your worksheet by using the Name Box.

   b. Use the **Chart Wizard** to create a basic pie chart that plots each daily activity as a percentage of the total time you spend on all of your activities during an average day.

   c. In **Step 2** of the Wizard, use the **Series** tab to select the appropriate **Category Labels** for your chart.

   d. In **Step 3**, choose a title for the chart, leave the legend displayed on the right, and show percent data labels.

   e. In **Step 4**, insert the chart into the current worksheet.

3. Move, resize, and format a chart:

   a. Move the chart so that it is centered below the data portion of the worksheet.

   b. Adjust the borders of the chart and the legend so that no chart elements obscure each other. Make any other size and placement adjustments that you think will improve the appearance of the chart.

   c. Change the chart's sub-type to a **3-D Exploded pie**.

   d. Increase the **elevation** of the pie by **thirty** degrees, and **rotate** it **twenty** degrees counter-clockwise.

   e. Change the color of the largest pie slice in the chart.

   f. Add a shadow to your chart's title and fill the title box with color.

4. Save and print the changes you have made to the spreadsheet:

   a. Save the file as **Test 4.xls**.

   b. Preview the worksheet and use the **Page Setup** dialog box to make it fit on one page if necessary.

   c. Print a copy of the entire worksheet.

   d. Print a copy of just the chart.

Excel 2000

Interactivity (continued)

Problem Solving

1. A friend of yours is considering learning Microsoft Excel. You want to convince your friend that the task is well worthwhile. In order to do this, you plan to show him or her the spreadsheets you have created while learning Excel. First, however, you decide to incorporate the latest techniques you have learned into the spreadsheets so that they are truly impressive. Return to the files Solved 2.xls and Solved 3-Grad.xls, and add at least one text box, one comment, and a chart to each. Use these features to call attention to and further illustrate important data in the worksheets. Be sure to save the additions you make to the files. Save the files as Solved 4.xls and Solved 4-Grad.xls.

2. Open the file Solved-HR3.xls, which you saved at the end of the previous lesson. Using the data you have already entered, create a 3D Pie chart to express graphically the distribution of the $10,000 that has been added to your Human Resources expense account. Also, add a text box that explains that the figures are proposals based on your preferences and projections. Then add two arrows – one that points from the text box to the chart, and one that points from the text box to the actual data. Print the worksheet and save the file as Solved-HR4.xls.

3. Open the file Solved-Rest3.xls, which you also saved at the end of the previous lesson. Insert a comment in the worksheet that lists all the ranges that the worksheet contains (if you do not have a cell labeled Ranges, add one and then insert the comment in this cell). Format the comment so that its background is Sky Blue and its text is Red. Then, add data to the worksheet, including appropriate labels and values, that details the pay scale at the restaurant. For example, include the pay rate earned by an employee with 0-6 months experience, 6-12 months experience, 12-18 months experience, etc. Finally, use the Chart Wizard to express this data with a Bar chart (use the Clustered Bar sub-type). Save the file as Solved-Rest4.xls and print a copy of just the chart.

4. Use Excel to create the worksheet below. You will need to make formatting changes to the chart once it is created.

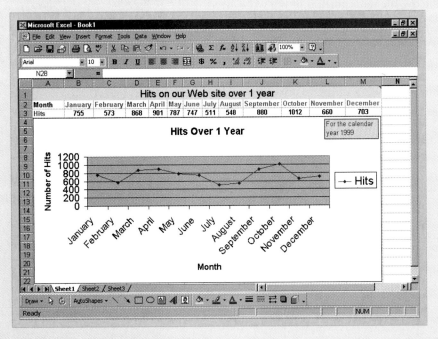

When you are finished, change the chart type to Stacked Column. Format the axis and series labels so that they are easy to read. Decide which chart type presents the data more effectively and keep that chart in the worksheet, changing back to the original if necessary. Save your file as Solved4-Hits.xls.

Glossary

A

Absolute cell reference
A cell reference that will remain fixed, even if the formula containing the reference is moved. To make a cell reference absolute, place a dollar sign ($), before both the column letter and row number.

Active cell
The currently selected cell on a worksheet, indicated by the cell pointer.

Alignment
The horizontal position of values or labels within a cell (for example, left, right, or center).

Anchor cells
The first and last cells in a cell range; the cells used to express a range address (for example, B9:E9).

Animated border
Indicates that a cell's contents have been sent to the Clipboard.

Answer Wizard tab
A Help tab that allows you to ask questions about Excel topics, much like the Office Assistant.

Argument
Information such as a cell address, range, or value, enclosed in parentheses, used by a function or macro to produce a result.

Arithmetic operators
Symbols used by Excel to perform formula calculations such as +,-,*, and /.

Assumption
A variable factor that is useful for conducting What-If analysis in a worksheet.

AutoCalculate box
Automatically displays the total of the values in a selected group of cells in the status bar.

AutoComplete
Automatically finishes entering a label when its first letter(s) match that of a label used previously in the column.

AutoFill
Automatically fills a range with series information such as the days of the week when the range after the first value is selected using the fill handle.

AutoFormat
Adds a predesigned set of formatting to selected ranges. AutoFormats can modify numbers, borders, fonts, patterns, alignment, and the height and width of rows and columns.

AutoSum
A function that automatically adds the values in the cells directly above or to the left of the active cell.

C

Cancel button
Removes the contents of a cell and restores the cell's previous contents if there were any; marked by an X on the Formula bar.

Cell
The space formed by the intersection of a row and a column; the basic unit of a worksheet.

Cell address
A cell's identification code, composed of the letter and number of the column and row that intersect to form the cell (for example, B22).

Cell pointer
The black rectangle that outlines the active cell.

Cell reference
A cell address used to refer to a cell in a formula. Cell references can be relative or absolute.

Chart
A graphic representation of values and their relationships, used to identify trends and contrasts in data.

Chart Wizard
A series of specialized dialog boxes that guide you through the creation or modification of a chart.

Check box
A small square box that allows you to turn a dialog box option on or off by clicking it.

Clipboard
A temporary storage area for cut or copied text or graphics. You can paste the contents of the Clipboard into any cell, worksheet, or even another application file. The Windows Clipboard holds a piece of information until it is replaced by another piece of data, or until the computer is shut down. The Office Clipboard holds up to twelve pieces of data at once and can be viewed as a toolbar.

Close
To quit an application and remove its window from the screen. You can also close a file while leaving the application open. The Close button appears in the upper-right corner of the application or worksheet window.

Column selector button
The grey rectangle that appears above each column and displays its column letter.

Comment
An electronic note that can be attached to a cell. Similar to a text box, but can be hidden from view.

Contents tab
A Help tab that organizes Excel's help files by topics and subtopics, much like the table of contents in a book or an outline.

Control menu
Contains commands relating to resizing, moving, and closing a window.

Copy
To place a duplicate of a file, or portion thereof, on the Clipboard to be pasted in another location.

Cut
To remove a file, or a portion of a file, and place it on the Clipboard.

D

Data series
The selected data taken from a worksheet and converted into a chart.

Delete
To remove the contents from a cell or an object such as a chart from the worksheet.

Dialog box
A box that offers additional command options for you to review or change before executing the command.

Documentation
The first section of a worksheet. It contains important information such as the spreadsheet's author, purpose, date of creation, file name, macros, and ranges.

Drawing toolbar
Contains tools for creating and formatting shapes, text boxes, and WordArt.

Dummy row/column
A blank row or column at the end of a defined range that holds a place so that Excel can recalculate formulas correctly if a new row or column is added to the range.

E

Edit
To add, delete, or modify cell contents or other elements of a file.

Electronic spreadsheet application
A computer program designed to organize information in columns and rows on a worksheet and facilitate performing rapid and accurate calculations on groups of interrelated numbers.

Ellipsis
Three dots (...) after a command that indicate a dialog box will follow with options for executing the command.

Enter button
Confirms cell entries. The Enter button is located on the Formula bar and is symbolized by a check mark.

Exploded pie slice
A pie chart slice that has been dragged away from the rest of the pie to emphasize it.

F

Fill handle
The small black square at the bottom right corner of the cell pointer. Draging the fill handle copies a cell's contents to adjacent cells or fills a range with series information.

Floating toolbar
A toolbar housed in its own window rather than along an edge of a window. All toolbars in Excel 2000 can be dragged to a floating position.

Folders
Subdivisions of a disk that function as a filing system to help you organize files.

Font
A name given to a collection of text characters of a certain size, weight, and style. Font has become synonymous with typeface. Arial and Times New Roman are examples of font names.

Format
The way information appears on a page. To format means to change the appearance of data without changing its content.

Formula
A combination of cell addresses and operators that instructs Excel to perform calculations such as adding, subtracting, multiplying, or averaging.

Formula bar
The area below the Formatting toolbar that displays cell contents whether they are labels, values, or formulas. You may enter and edit cell contents in the formula bar rather than in the cell itself.

Function
A built-in formula included in Excel that makes it easy for you to perform common calculations.

G

Go To
A useful command for moving great distances across a worksheet.

Gridlines
Vertical and horizontal lines on a chart that delineate a cell's boundaries.

I

Index
A Help tab that lists all of Excel's help topics alphabetically.

Input
The data you enter into a worksheet and work with to produce results.

Insertion point
A vertical blinking line on the screen that indicates where text and graphics will be inserted. The insertion point also indicates where an action will begin.

L

Label
Text or numbers that describe the data you place in rows and columns. Labels should be entered in a worksheet first to define the rows and columns and are automatically left-aligned by Excel.

Label prefix
A typed character that marks an entry as a label. For example, if you type an apostrophe before a number, it will be treated as label rather than as a value.

Landscape
A term used to refer to horizontal page orientation; opposite of "portrait," or vertical, orientation.

Launch
To start a program so you can work with it.

Legend
The section of a chart that details which colors or patterns on a chart represent which information.

M

Macro
A set of instructions that automates a specific multistep task that you perform frequently, reducing the process to one command.

Menu
A list of related application commands.

Menu bar
Lists the names of menus containing application commands. Click a menu name on the menu bar to display its list of commands.

Merge and Center command
Combines two or more adjacent cells into a single cell and places the contents of the upper left-most cell at the center of the new cell.

Mouse pointer
The usually arrow-shaped cursor on the screen that you control by guiding the mouse on your desk. You use the mouse pointer to select items, drag objects, choose commands, and start or exit programs. The shape of the mouse pointer can change depending on the task being executed.

N

Name Box
The box at the left end of the Formula bar that displays the address of the active cell or the name of a selected range that has been defined and named. You can also use the drop-down arrow in the Name Box to select a named range.

O

Object
An item such as a chart or graphic that that can be relocated and resized independently of the structure of the worksheet.

Office Assistant
An animated representation of the Microsoft Office 2000 help facility. The Office Assistant provides hints, instructions, and a convenient interface between the user and Excel's various help features.

Open
Command used to access a file that has already been created and saved on disk.

Order of operations
The order Excel follows when calculating formulas with multiple operations: 1) exponents, 2) multiplication and division from left to right, 3) addition and subtraction from left to right. In addition, operations inside parenthesis are calculated first, using the above order.

Output
The results produced by calculations done on the input data of a worksheet.

P

Paste
To insert cut or copied data into other cells, worksheets, or workbooks.

Paste Function command
Command that allows you to choose and perform a calculation without entering its formula on the keyboard.

Paste Special command
Allows you to paste the contents of a cell using formatting characteristics that you specify.

Personal Macro Workbook
Allows you to store macros so that they will be available to all Excel workbooks.

Point size
A measurement used for the size of text characters and row height. There are 72 points in 1 inch.

Portrait
A term used to refer to vertical page orientation; opposite of "landscape," or horizontal, orientation.

Print Preview
Allows you to view your worksheet as it will appear when printed on a sheet of paper.

Program
A software application that performs specific tasks, such as Microsoft Word or Microsoft Excel.

Programs menu
A menu on the Windows 95 or 98 Start menu that lists the applications on your computer such as Microsoft Excel.

R

Radio button
A small circular button in a dialog box that allows you to turn options on or off.

RAM (random access memory)
The memory that programs use to function while the computer is on. When you shut down the computer, all information in RAM is lost.

Range
A group of two or more cells, usually adjacent.

Range name
A name chosen for a selected group of cells that describes the data they contain.

Relative cell reference
Allows a formula to be moved to a new location on a worksheet. The formula will then follow the same directional instructions from the new starting point using new cell references.

Reviewing toolbar
Contains commands for inserting, deleting, displaying, and navigating between comments.

Right-click
To click the right mouse button; often used to access specialized menus and shortcuts.

Row height
The measurement of a cell from top to bottom.

Row selector button
The grey rectangle that appears to the left of each row and displays its row number.

Run
To start an application. Also refers to initiating the steps of a macro.

S

Save
Stores changes you have made to a file maintaining the file's current name and location.

Save As
Command used to save a new file for the first time or to create a duplicate copy of a file that has already been saved.

ScreenTip
A brief explanation of a button or object that appears when the mouse pointer is paused over it. Other ScreenTips are accessed by using the What's This? feature on the Help menu or by clicking the question mark button in a dialog box.

Scroll bar
A graphical device for moving vertically and horizontally through a document with the mouse. Scroll bars are located along the right and bottom edges of the document window.

Scroll bar box

A small grey box located inside a scroll bar that indicates your current position relative to the rest of the document window. You can advance a scroll bar box by dragging it, clicking the scroll bar on either side of it, or by clicking the scroll arrows.

Sizing handles

Small squares on the corners and sides of a selected object that can be used for changing its dimensions.

Select All button

The grey rectangle in the upper-left corner of the worksheet where the row and column headings meet. Clicking the Select All button highlights the entire worksheet.

Series of labels

A range of incremental labels created by entering the first label in the series and then dragging the fill handle the number of cells desired. Excel automatically enters the remaining labels in order.

Sheet

The term Excel uses to refer to an individual worksheet (Sheet 1, Sheet 2, etc.).

Sheet tab scrolling buttons

Allow you to access Sheet tabs that are not visible in the window. An Excel workbook opens with only 3 worksheets, but you may use 255 per workbook.

Status bar

Displays information regarding your current activity in Excel such as when a cell is ready for editing and when the Number Lock is activated.

Start

To open an application for use.

Start button

A button on the taskbar that accesses a special menu that you use to start programs, find files, access Windows Help and more.

T

Taskbar

A bar, usually located at the bottom of the screen, that contains the Start button, shows which programs are running by displaying their program buttons, and shows the current time.

Text box

A rectangular area in which text is added so that it may be manipulated independently of the rest of a document.

Title bar

The horizontal bar at the top of a window that displays the name of the document or application that appears in the window.

Toolbar

A graphical bar containing buttons that act as shortcuts for common commands.

V

Values

The numbers, formulas, and functions that Excel uses to perform calculations.

W

What-If analysis

Technique by which you change certain conditions in a worksheet to see how the changes affect the results of your spreadsheet output.

Window
A rectangular area on the screen in which you view and work on files.

Workbook
An Excel file made up of related worksheets. An individual workbook may contain up to 255 worksheets.

Worksheet
The workspace made up of columns and rows where you enter data to create an electronic spreadsheet.

Worksheet tab
The markers near the bottom of the window that identify which worksheet is currently active. To open a different worksheet, click its tab. Worksheet tabs can be named to reflect their contents.

X

X-axis label
A label summarizing the horizontal (x-axis) data on a chart.

Y

Y-axis label
A label summarizing the vertical (y-axis) data on a chart.

Index

X